WORK 2.0
NOWHERE TO HIDE

SERGIUSZ PROKURAT

Publisher: University of Euroregional Economy

Printed in the United States of America

Printed by CS, North Charleston, SC

2013

Book release date: 2nd of December 2013. Price in US is 9.99 USD.

Publisher's Cataloging-in-Publication data:

Prokurat, Sergiusz.
    Work 2.0 : nowhere to hide / written and illustrated by Sergiusz
Prokurat.
    p. cm.
    Includes bibliographic references.
    ISBN 978-1-4922-5246-7
1. Economics–Future Trends 2. Economics–Impact of Advanced
Technology on 3. Technological Unemployment 4. Job satisfaction 5.
Organizational change I. Title.

Available on Amazon, Kindle, B&N, B&T, and other book stores

ISBN-10: 1492252468
ISBN-13: 978-1492252467
Library of Congress Control Number (LCCN): 2013921119

Book has a dedicated website:
work-2-0.com

CONTENTS

SERGIUSZ PROKURAT

Your work is going to fill a large part of your life, and the only way to be truly satisfied is to do what you believe is great work. And the only way to do great work is to love what you do. If you haven't found it yet, keep looking. Don't settle. As with all matters of the heart, you'll know when you find it.

Steve Jobs

SERGIUSZ PROKURAT

PREFACE

We're living through a dramatic revolution. Ten years ago, there was no such thing as Facebook. Ten years before that, we didn't have Amazon or the Web. New technologies have opened up new opportunities. They bring with them an ever more complex reality. Growing complexity is a process caused by globalisation, technology and progress–a broader set of activities, more departments in companies, more workers, more processes to service, all of these provoke a continuous rise in the number of functioning procedures, new policies and rules. They bring about the phenomenon of extreme worker specialisation (also known as hyperspecialisation). This calls for a different approach to management and work. For some time now we've observed a greater focus on flexibility, mobility, and the ability of quick adaptation of workers. The world of work is in evolution.

You have to know that globalisation cannot be stopped. After work we sit down with our computers and look for products on the internet without considering location. We like to shop cheaply. But we don't always like to manufacture cheaply. In such a situation government budgets and our pockets can't possibly be balanced. This is the problem the West is currently facing. People still want to buy things, but they're often out of work and consequently lack the money to do so. This is a significant fact, as today we don't compare our production or industrial capabilities with a neighbouring country as before, but with a manufacturer from China, Taiwan, Indonesia or India. We see the inhabitants of these countries on TV and still can't believe that they're so close… right next to us, thanks to technology.

When we look at the business realities of the 21st century such as a decentralised work force and companies which leverage both networks and communities, we see opportunities for a more rapid pace of innovation, more efficiency in production and a truly global market for products. A special part of making this happen has been the rise of Web 2.0, which has provided millions of people all over the world with the ability of to influence thoughts and behaviour on a global scale. It might not be an exaggeration to state that one person could bring about a revolution. We can now attract people who think alike and build support for our ideas and actions. We have the ability to gather as never before to brainstorm, voice our opinions and think about solutions. We can interact with people thousands of miles away as if they were in the other room. Our voice can be heard regardless of location and context, and this is what makes social media a truly powerful phenomenon.

But technology is a double-edged sword, as it has the ability to both liberate and enslave. Technology is changing the nature of work, enriching us, and as companies redefine how and where different tasks are carried out, they require new skills and new employer-employee relationships. However, jobs for workers others than the global hyper-skilled or hyper-connected elite are disappearing—this transformation is leaving many people without a job for good. Globalisation continues to suppress the future income of those who still haven't started working. World 2.0 is approaching, while in countries which were formerly considered rich, people are losing jobs due to automation or the shift to low-cost locations. The result of this globalisation is that there is a huge surplus of labour supply - a vast army of people who are out of work, with little money or prospects. The majority, in terms of job security and availability has suffered badly. The stats you can find in this book clearly show a huge amount of wealth flowing up to the top 1% and the bottom 80% falling behind dramatically, a drop in employment, and youth fresh out of school with no job prospects because they don't know how to navigate this new world which has its own brand new set of rules. The global youth is becoming unemployed and discouraged.

Work will ultimately return. But it won't be the same kind of work as before. China is under immense pressure, and cash is flowing out of all emerging markets, Europe is experiencing huge tensions, so no one is really surprised that global growth is sluggish at best. However, a small group of insightful economic thinkers suggest that our current situation isn't temporary, but the start of a completely new cycle of slower growth. Their reasoning is as follows: our work will be done by computer programmes, apps basically, while we need to learn how to use them, how to change the way we build relationships, and how to engage in online communities. No one is going to pay you a salary just for showing up at work. Employers will have new expectations for their workers, thus creating a more flexible, more freelance, more collaborative and far less secure world of work. It will be run by people with new values, driven by the coming of Work 2.0.

The old employment system of secure, lifelong jobs with predictable advancement and stable pay is dead. It's time for Work 2.0. There is nowhere to hide. Resistance is futile and eventually all of us will be assimilated.

CHAPTER 1: THE TRANSFORMATION

Nearly all economists from the classical or neoclassical school of thought, which traces its origins to Adam Smith, assumed that the three basic factors of production are land, capital and labour. In time, however, this began to change. Modern society, whose birth we are now experiencing in the highly advanced countries of the Western world, is in the process of dynamic transformation, and so too are the methods of wealth creation. Consequently, capitalism itself is evolving, because in essence it is a system of accumulating wealth. Mass production, which for the many years of the Fordist era has been the main source of income for companies and the main source of employment is being replaced by new ways of creating value based on services, therefore on entrepreneurship, knowledge and innovativeness.

Changes in the global economy bring with them changes in the structure of employment. In developed countries an increasing share of the economic structure belongs not to agriculture, nor to industrial production, but to services. Today the so-called most industrialised countries in the world are, paradoxically, economies based on service industries. In fact economies are often compared by this metric, with the idea being that a larger share of services implies an economically more advanced country.

Today it is knowledge which is becoming the prime production factor, and although this doesn't diminish the role of capital, undoubtedly, knowledge is coming into its own right. This is happening because thanks to the knowledge one has the skills and experience acquired in many deployments, we can transform the raw data of any company into information which is useful for its business. Have you ever wondered how much information is worth? Paradoxically, information is a stronger weapon than many conventional types of arms. Every person is in fact a medium of information. We have direct influence on the content created, and we also make information public. We are responsible for the message, which in turn creates a certain reaction.

Knowledge is becoming the most important source of competitive advantage (Thurow, 1996: 81). This is possible thanks to new information technologies, whose development has paramount importance for countries' socio-economic systems. It is due to this transformation that in the US from the 1990s an increasing share of investment is classified as intangible investments (Figure 1). Although they already implement and provide individuals with the power of advanced technology and a network full of rich multimedia content, new digital tools are still very much in the experimental phase (the internet's „golden age" is barely a decade old), many signs seem to indicate that we are witnessing a transformation as described by Peter F. Drucker – the economic, social and moral landscape of the world is changing (1994). According to the data, as recently as December 1996 internet access was a privilege enjoyed by only 36 million people, which amounted to 0.6% of global population (data source: IDC). In June 2001 the number of internet users had risen to 479 million (Nua Ltd data). Five years later the web was used by 1 billion, 43 million people (Internet World Stats data) – 16% of the Earth's

Figure 1. US Private Industry Investments (as % of output)

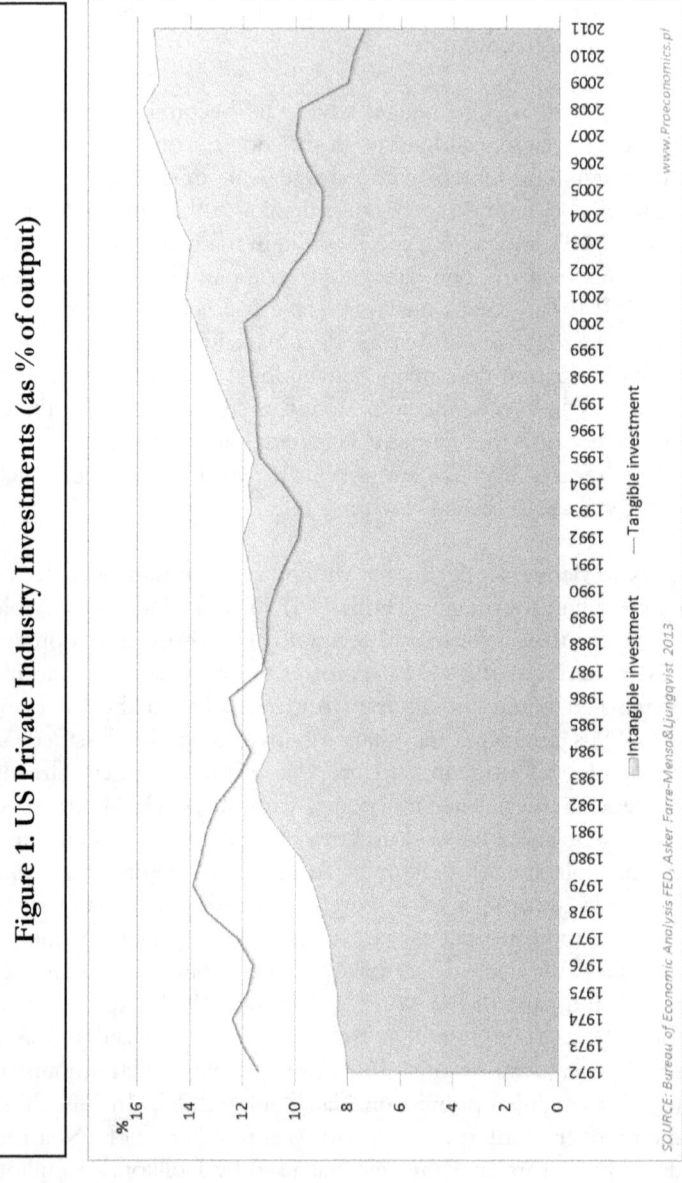

SOURCE: Bureau of Economic Analysis FED, Asker Farre-Mensa&Ljungqvist 2013

www.Proeconomics.pl

Intangible investment —Tangible investment

inhabitants. Yet the real acceleration was still to follow. In June 2011 2 billion people had internet access (30.4%) (Internet World Stats data). At the time of writing, in March 2013, the internet claims 2.749 billion users (38.8%) (I.T.U data). The web is everywhere and it's the vanguard of globalisation. New technology enables a new society.

This transformation is slowly changing interpersonal relations, society, culture and politics. It influences the way economic and social institutions work, the way we understand technology, human freedom, and it also influences the way we define ourselves. Peter Drucker, who coined the term 'knowledge-based economy', thinks that we're living through a transformation into a post-capitalist society. In his opinion currently knowledge is mainly used to process knowledge. In essence, possessing knowledge enables you to detect how existing knowledge can be best used to achieve the results we're aiming for. Knowledge is systematically and deliberately used to determine what kind of new knowledge is required, is it already available and what must be done to make it effective. In other words, knowledge is used to introduce breakthrough innovations. Simply speaking, innovation is all about introducing and creating new or newly-combined market links, which unlock previously unknown growth prospects. One of these possible links is a novel use of a resource which wasn't even considered a resource until an entrepreneur (or any person for that matter) found a use for it. Often this new resource didn't have any attributed value beforehand (thus weed „becomes" a plant, and a stone „becomes" a mineral). It is innovation itself which seems to be the distinctive element of a post-industrial society's economic system.

Capturing the core changes is still a challenge. It's not enough to state that the most prominent feature of a post-industrial society is knowledge and the processing of knowledge. As stated by B. Laurel, human integration with computers takes place when simultaneously three actions-sensations merge: sensory immersion in the new world and strong sensory arousal, remote presence, and increasingly so, teleoperations. These three elements are, in essence, the human response to the digital world (1993). We have learned to interact with computers and immensely complicated data, efficiently visualising and manipulating them. Soon computers will become complementary to our existence and our personality – they will foresee our expectations, substitute our memory, and they may even complement our thought process. Our cognitive potential: mind, memory and observational capacity will be expanded and assisted by the computing power of processors. Our physical presence will be supplemented by digital beings (e.g. our avatars developed in MMORGs, our presence in the world of Second Life, our interactions on our favourite forums) which will represent us in cyberspace. Many terms such as „interface" will be consigned to the annals of history – we will become fully integrated with the world of the Web. As people are also computers – it is the unchanging hardware (the „brain"), not the contingent software („thoughts"), that is seen as the locus of human essence (Fisher, 2010: 159) – everything will come down to skills and the ability of adaptation. Even physically we are slowly becoming cyborgs (a combination of man and machine) – especially when we stare into our computer screen. Artificial prostheses allow disabled people to walk, while mobile phones greatly expand the range of our hearing. Laptops give us access to the source of mass intelligence, which is in essence an extension of our brain. Facebook, from an anthropological point of view, constitutes artificial intelligence, which we can constantly access. We solve problems using it (where to see a movie? what to wear?). Thus this changes the way we function and work on an everyday basis. In a decade or so, after the complete unification of the real and virtual realities, we will enter a world of digitally-created reality, where information will be all around us. Everything points to the fact that World 2.0 will be an environment of digital access to knowledge.

Regardless of how exactly our world will look like in a dozen years or so, technology will leave its mark on the media, information consumers, content, and on how we will work.

The internet has become a space where anyone who is connected can make a place for himself. This aspect is actively building a new type of society. With the spread of the new digital economy, an industrial society is being replaced by an advanced knowledge society, also known as the information society. The new economy is strongest where technological implementation is most advanced. According to Anthony Giddens the US is the place where the economy based on creativity has directly affected nearly half of all paid salaries (2007).

All these changes are influencing the way we understand the concept of 'work'. We're starting to change the way we perceive its boundaries, scope and nature. Jack Nilles, the creator of the concept of teleworking and telecommuting, said that people shouldn't commute to work, but rather work should reach people (Bellido, 2006: 27). Teleworking is a concept which arose at the beginning of the 1970s during the US oil crisis, and meant work done outside the usual place of work and remotely by using technical communication media and a computer. Meanwhile Work 2.0 is a broader term. The main motive of implementing teleworking was reducing road traffic, while Work 2.0 is the effect of a technological revolution and the creation of the digital world.

The transformation which is currently taking shape had been envisaged by futurologist Alvin Toffler. In his 1980 book „The Third Wave" he writes about the idea of an information society, where people work from home (Toffler, 1980). The core concept of his Third Wave was teleworking, which would gradually destroy traditional work spaces. Why? Because technological progress is impossible to stop. Toffler also noted that the influence news has on people is undergoing an evident change. The range of information which a person has access to is expanding. Information, processed in thousands of ways, penetrates all areas of life, brings people and economies all over the world together, leads to creating new machines, programmes and computer applications and leads to decentralisation. Never before, according to Toffler, in any civilisation did we have such powerful tools (1980). The waves of economic development were also foreseen by others. An interesting example of the economic system's evolution can be found in the work of J. Schumpeter (1934) and his followers C. Freeman and L. Soete (1997: 58). In this context transformation is presented as incoming subsequent waves with each wave shorter than its predecessor, which implies a quicker pace of change and a more frequent appearance of key inventions. Each of the waves begins with a breakthrough innovation, which changes the established system of producing goods and services and introduces revolutionary changes in all aspects of life.

Table 1. Five Technological Waves which have Changed our World

First Wave	Second Wave	Third Wave	Fourth Wave	Fifth Wave
1750	1850	1900	1950	2000
water energy textiles iron	steam energy railroads steel	electricity chemicals internal combustion engine	petro-chemistry electronics flight	internet digital networks software new media

source: author's research

The first wave which irrevocably changed the world is linked to the creation of the first blast furnaces in England and the use of J. Kay's flying shuttle in the weaving industry in combination with steam power (1760 – the Industrial Revolution in England). The second wave is related to the widespread use of the steam engine, invented by J. Watt, in many sectors of the economy. This invention led to the rapid development of the rail network, which enabled better communication and shortened the time needed to move people and goods. The third wave came about with the invention of the light bulb and internal combustion engine. These products changed industry, led to the development of new industries and improved those which had already existed. The fourth wave can be described as applying knowledge to already existing products, such as airplanes. Also entirely new industries were created such as the production of computer components and modern electronic equipment. Finally, the fifth wave is the transformation we are currently living through, brought about by the invention of digital networks and the internet. New products based on new technologies, such as social networks, were created. The internet minimised the time taken by information to flow and distance ceased to play a role in business contacts. The further intensification of this wave depends on adequate economic and social conditions (not everyone has internet access), including conducive social attitudes, high quality of human capital and a significant role played by the state in creating the administrative, legal and institutional preconditions for the development of science and entrepreneurship.

The story of the internet began as early as the 1950s. It was then that, thanks to innovations resulting from a combination of military strategy, advanced science, technological entrepreneurship and counter-culture activity, the first seeds of the web were planted, which in time grew and covered the whole world. At last data could be gathered, processed and saved without the use of a central unit. Global communication became reality. In March 1989 Tim Berners-Lee and Robert Cailliau dreamt up a project of creating a web of hypertext documents called the World Wide Web (www). This was to be a collection of hypertext documents. In December 1990 Tim Berners-Lee created the basics of HTML and the first web page. Two years later the first graphic web browser called Mosaic was written.

Yet the goals of the creators of the global web were very different from those one might expect. In principle the internet was to be used for remote calculations using computers distributed over a large area, which would lead to significant savings in energy and time. Yet most users didn't need so much computing power, besides that, they weren't prepared to adapt their computers to the requirements of such operations. However, what did capture the attention of people was the possibility of communicating on an unprecedented scale. This is how the most popular (to this day) use of the internet emerged – the internet as a mass inter-human communication tool (Castells, 1996).

We search for the bus schedule, rate restaurants, and download MP3s online, but we work in the traditional world. We take the bus to work, while during our time off we pop out for some lunch, and listen to the MP3s we downloaded when returning home. We currently live in a hybrid world, where the traditional world coexists with its digital counterpart. Despite this we are in the midst of the next wave of socio-economic development, name it as we may. A. Toffler called it the transition to the information society; D. Bell reckoned it was the post-industrial phase (1973: 57). J. Naisbitt is of the opinion that the correct name is the knowledge society (1982). P. Drucker in turn uses the term post-capitalist society (1994: 1). Also concepts such as 'digital economy' or 'network economy', 'information society', 'information economy' have been mentioned. The philosopher Z. Bauman terms it 'liquid modernity', i.e. a world which is a continuation and simultaneously the opposite of a stable modernity.

The name 'global village', used with regard to the modern world, ceases to be just a metaphor, because technologies make our world flat to a degree we've never seen before. Consequently Thomas Friedman is right to suddenly exclaim that in the 21st century „holy mackerel, the world is flat" (2005). This flattened or flat world, besides all its pros, also has its cons, as illustrated by the following joke:

The dialogue takes place during an exam at a university. The professor asks a student.
- What do you know about the current economic situation?
- I'm afraid I can't answer that question.
- So maybe something about the upcoming elections?
The student doesn't say a word.
- Please could you describe the economic outlook for our country?
- I don't know anything about it.
- Maybe something then related to the fight against global warming?
No answer.
- Please tell me where are you from? – the professor asks gently.
- My parents came here from a small village on the coast of Mexico.
The professor, without saying a word, paces towards the window and for a very long time stares straight ahead looking through the window. Finally he takes a deep breath and says to himself:
- Why not just quit all this damn stuff and go to the beach in Mexico?

Everyone, sometimes, would just like to quit everything and drive away - as far as possible - to find a place free of all the problems, phones ringing, constantly arriving emails, meetings, difficult conversations, and acquaintances in your social networks. As recently as two decades ago this was all possible. Now your smartphone, your work tool, is always with you, and thus our friends and acquaintances are always close. Using Facebook we can always tell them what we're up to – all of them at the same time. We have in our pockets a mobile communication system, including a GPS and a dozen or so books, just in case. We're „transparently available". Marc Zuckerberg, the creator of Facebook and supporter of radical transparency, thinks that there's no place for privacy in the 21st century.

The transformation of our life, work, leisure and thinking is changing society's culture. M. Castells states that „technology is society and society cannot be understood and represented without its technological tools" (1996: 5). The information society can be described by an exponential increase of productivity, a high degree of media interference, the domination of information production factors over the content being transmitted, and dependency of the many aspects of social life on receiving and producing information. In such a society knowledge becomes a commodity – the role of specialists and scientists is even more important than before, because knowledge is the key source of innovation. However, this has its consequences. As knowledge becomes a commodity, so too does work. To a certain degree work has always been a commodity, but the labour market is not very transparent or flexible, to such a point that before it. Used to be much more efficient to hire someone permanently than use external co-operators – communication costs were just too high. Now, however, this transformation is a significant challenge for the labour market – both from the point of view of individual workers, who have to approach their role in a more flexible way, and also from the point of view of organisations, which are facing a radical transition.

CHAPTER 2: WORLD 2.0 AND THE CHANGING LABOUR MARKET

In 1980, if you wanted to buy a book first you'd have to pay the bus fare, leave home, get on the bus, drive all the way to the area where the bookstore was located, enter the store and buy the book (if it was available and you had a sufficient amount of money, because you didn't know the price beforehand). All this took you half a day and was only possible if the bookstore was open, which implied a trip during business hours (and what if you wanted to buy a book after work?). This process became even more complicated when what you wanted was a foreign book which was unavailable in the local bookstore. Currently most books can be bought in under a minute with just a few clicks via any device connected to the internet. Modern B2C systems implemented in internet stores automatically suggest the right choice for us and present us with other books which we may like. We can also see community ratings and reviews – all written by people who've already bought this book. Yet the revolution doesn't lie in our ability of doing this – technological progress was always about the increasing effectiveness of actions relative to the time consumed. The real revolution is defined by our new-found ability to not only be a passive consumer, but also an active participant in creating culture, which is the essence of the new era of World 2.0.

The term 2.0 is derived mainly from Web 2.0, a concept coined by Tim O'Reilly in 2004 (O'Reilly and Battelle, 2004; O'Reilly, 2005) and commonly used today to describe the next stage of development of many social areas (Web 2.0, Culture 2.0, Company 2.0, Science 2.0 etc.). Despite what might be suggested by the software numeral, Web 2.0 isn't a new World Wide Web (WWW) or the internet, but a different way of using its resources. The role of the web is evident – without it World 2.0 can't possibly exist. Examples of Web 2.0 include social networking   sites, blogs, wikis, folksonomies, videosharing sites, hosted services, web applications. Many people are of the opinion that Web 2.0 is changing the interaction paradigm between the owners of a website or service and its users, with most of content creation shifting to the users:

„Web 2.0 is a true business revolution in the computer world, caused by the shift towards the internet as a platform and the intent to understand the rules which govern it. The main rule is: Create applications which will better harness the web and thus more people will use them." (O'Reilly, 2005)

Web 2.0 is a system which does away with the old model of centralised websites and shifts the power of the web/internet to the user. Thus thanks to new technologies we receive a tool of creative expression with the ability of simultaneous reception and activity. This is a major shift which brings about mass participation in culture and social life. This is because new media aren't just means of communication but also serve as material for expression. This development 'wave', whose beginnings can be traced to 2001, can be best described as going from a 'read-only' (or downloading) web to a phase of active participation and value creation by the users (read and write, downloading and uploading). This is a difference as great as between active and passive use of media – between consumption and creation. Billions of individuals connected to the web can actively participate on a grass-roots level and together with companies or other organisations, in the process of creating innovative products and services, in acquiring wealth and contributing to countries' economic development in a way which as recently as three decades ago was completely impossible. Not without good reason did J. Rifkin write that the 21st century is a „new age of participation".

When I worked for the Polish edition of *Harvard Business Review* I had the opportunity to interview Andrew McAfee, who was kind enough to provide a couple of interesting insights about World 2.0. Its most important feature is that everyone is connected via the web with everyone else. We have developed technologies which not only allow us to interact with each other, but they also free us of the need of defining these interactions beforehand. In other words, the tools of Web 2.0 have a very interesting common denominator – thanks to them people get closer to each other while shedding the traditional rigidities of hierarchies, social roles or physical distance – they can create groups, communities, networks, or taskforces. A second new aspect is the fact that technologies related to artificial intelligence have been greatly improved over the last 10 years. Thus, for the first time we have computers which actually understand what we say to them, understand what we're asking and quickly and accurately answer these queries. This is still a very new phenomenon yet it's incredibly powerful – McAfee reassured. But someone might say – yes, but…. that doesn't really have any impact on me, I don't really use all that. – But that's just plain wrong! How wrong would such a person be? Let me explain by quoting Amy Shuen:

„You are already an integral part of Web 2.0 business economy. Every time you click on Google, Wikipedia, eBay or Amazon you are sparking network effect… even if you do not buy anything." (Shuen, 2008)

So why do people embrace the change? What do they actually get in return? Basically these changes allow them to work better. Productivity increases. They can solve problems more quickly than before. They can enter the stock market more quickly. They can find good co-workers. In short, these changes help people in their work.

How does it work? In World 2.0 it's the users who create value by creating user generated content – their feedback, comments, opinions, and reviews are priceless. Let's take blogs – according to Technorati, as recently as June 2001 there was only about 10 thousand, in March 2003 this number had already grown to 1 million, March 2005 saw 10 million blogs, while in August 2007 this number shot up to 85 million. Nowadays everyone can have a blog – all you need is to put in some effort, do some blogging and start creating value for your readers. If we create a community, commenters will appreciate our efforts, they will deem us value creators, they will get to know us and our ideas too, they will also pass on this value, which will in time cause the market to identify us. And the market can pay.

World 2.0 is an intangible, virtual and digital IT reality. It is there where the phenomenon I call 'ConsumeIT!' takes place. In short, ConsumeIT! is the fact of consuming culture through IT as enabled by the internet - something we've all experienced in our personal and social lives and in the numerous online facilities that have reshaped how we communicate, collaborate, learn, buy, engage and consume (Frank and Moore, 2010). The digital revolution is slowly replacing the traditional world. We'd rather consume culture through the digital world. To take just one example traditional books are becoming a „slowly fading relic of the printed word culture. Publishing technology is changing rapidly and the work of a writer can nowadays be shared in the form of journalism, literature, art, photography, music, film and video in multimedia and interactive forms. Producing these newer forms costs much less than the traditional process of book publishing, hence the large popularity of audiobooks, to mention just one phenomenon. In the US audiobooks are taking over the market – there are over 100 thousand titles available right now. Every year a dozen or so thousand new audiobooks are published, mostly new editions of books which achieved success in the traditional form. The American audiobook market is growing at a pace far greater than that of traditional books also because their particular purpose is different – they're most commonly listened to in the car, often during the ride to work. Audiobooks are also popular in Western Europe, where their most common use is for home listening; this is what 85% of British consumers do.

ConsumeIT has also taken over the music industry. The internet is awash with shops offering CDs which are sent to the purchaser by post or courier. There are also many stores offering music in digital form (e.g. MP3). Rather than going to a physical store, a consumer logs on to a website, where he can read a review of the recordings, listen to certain samples and buy music. Thus the shop is virtual, but the product itself is unchanged – after receiving the shipment or downloading the file, the consumer is the proud owner of the same disc which he could have bought in a physical or traditional location. From the point of view of the music industry the change mostly affects the last link of the distribution chain – the retail merchant, i.e. the place of the music store or supermarket is taken by an internet store. This form of purchase is attractive mainly due to its price – music recording (CDs are obsolete, though coming back in the retro market) in some cases are even 50% cheaper than in traditional stores. And besides internet stores there's an increasing number of stores which offer online music, which means eliminating the medium, usually a CD, and replacing it with a computer file. These examples are evidence of the 'revolution', which has taken place and is still taking place in the channels we use to access culture. There have already been cases of publishing music without the help of a music label company, which reduces the cost of the record for the end consumer. For example the New York-based band GrooveLily has a policy of distributing its records uniquely online. That is also how they communicate with their fans.

To sum up the above ConsumeIT has given us access to a broad range of goods. The economy we're currently creating is a very rich economy--an economy of prosperity and abundance, with immediate access to the whole culture mankind has created throughout centuries. Thanks to ConsumeITwe can freely navigate time and space. We don't have to go to Rometo see its sights. Google enables us to see the Coliseum or use 3D simulations. For amateurs of niche cultural offerings, classic Norwegian films are available online with English subtitles.

All this leads us to conclude that an individual participating in this virtual life won't eventually need his or her real environment anymore – all behaviour patterns or ways of reacting to reality will be learned and discovered online. The world of ConsumeIT provides us with most things we could possibly want. A special example of this virtual world is the game Second Life. This relatively internet phenomenon, which nevertheless offers a glimpse into the future of social relations, is populated by several million users, a virtual world, with its society, economy and politics, which are starting to mirror reality. What if someone would value their virtual life more than real life? Some criticise the culture born out of the new internet reality by saying that it's basically the dumpsite of civilisation, leading to a loss of respect for culture, characterised by a lack of professionalism, a cult of amateurs, mediocrity and lack of competence. Whether or not we agree with this accusation, say the critics, soon uniformity will encompass everyone and everything – and then there won't be any reason for complaining at all. Obviously the world of Web 2.0 complicates a great deal of things, invalidating existing standards without creating new ones. True, the internet destroys many things! Yet it has more in common with the logic of creative destruction, described by economist Joseph Schumpeter, the patron saint of the digital era – the internet destroys in order to rebuild stronger and more effective structures.

The development of mass media, including the internet, has caused huge changes in the distribution of culture and in the way people communicate with each other. Granted, as is the case of every change, this change isn't only a threat, as mentioned above, but most of all an enormous chance for innovators. It provides new opportunities for building the competitive advantage of products, new types of brands, new distribution channels and new advertising. For instance the concept of „Marketing 3.0" is all about using new ways of communicating and elements of social responsibility, as described by the undisputed marketing guru Philip Kotler. In its essence this phenomenon hinges on using the fact, that „consumers have realised, that their purchasing power has global effects, which has influenced their behaviour and the need of voicing their opinion about the choices they make". Marketing 3.0 can also be characterised by the fact that in business you can „use community discussions, position your brand as a positive force which is changing the world and cooperate with consumers who are also brand advocates or champions". These new brands not only meet the basic needs of the consumer but also „fight poverty, initiate socio-cultural change and influence the protection of the natural environment" (Kotler, Kartajaya and Setiawan, 2010).

Figure 2. Communication in World 2.0

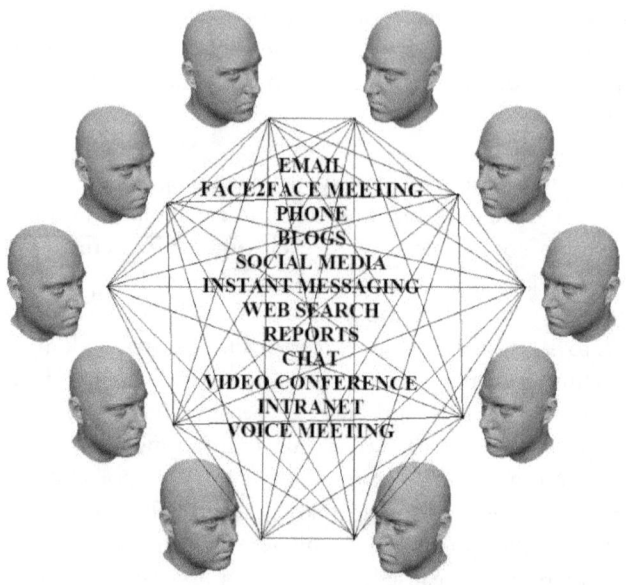

The most important features of World 2.0 are:

Interactivity. World 2.0 offers its users an unprecedented possibility of interacting and integration – an unlimited exchange of ideas. This is because internet services have the user at their core. The tools of the traditional internet from World 1.0 didn't allow for full interaction in the digital world and didn't offer the option of ConsumeIT. Although a website or service is usually prepared by certain authors or creators, the core of its functioning is based on users, who experience content and exchange this content P2P. Virtual user communities are created around certain issues, and these communities start cooperating, interacting, and constructing a network of contacts. Opinion and experience exchange intensifies. One portal suddenly is not enough. On Facebook commenters paste links to Google Plus and communicate this on Twitter, not only using their computers but also smartphones and tablets. In 2013 over half of the global internet user network (51%) uses Facebook, with 25% simultaneously declaring themselves as Google Plus users, while 22% uses Twitter and YouTube (GlobalWebIndex, 2013). Interactivity enables the user to control the information which reaches him - interactions are defined as mutual influence of people, objects, phenomena; an encounter of two or more actions, behaviours, aspirations; it's a process of communication which causes individuals to modify their behaviour. Because information in the digital world spills over from one medium to another, with no control, interactivity in the world of Web 2.0 can provide huge power.

"Central to Web 2.0 is the requirement for interactive systems to enable the participation of users in production and social interaction. Consequently, in order to critically explore the Web 2.0 phenomenon it is important to explore the relationship of interactivity to social power." (Jarrett, 2008)

Simultaneity. In Web 2.0 each computer is both client and server at the same time. This causes the previously distinct roles of sender and receiver to blur – anyone can be one and the other – this phenomenon has been called 'sendceiving' (sending and receiving). The internet enables us to immediately access the entire history of the world and we can also make history as we go. This has profoundly changed the concepts of time and space.

Any user can belong to many communities at the same time and can simultaneously engage in many conversations and use many applications (multitasking). We can perform research on the internet, listen to music and communicate at the same time. Such behaviour is in clear contrast to the traditional philosophical or educational positions demanding 'concentration'. In 1999 only 16% of people from the 8-18 age range used more than one medium at the same time.

Meanwhile in 2009 this percentage rose to 29%, according to the report „Generation M2: Media in the Lives of 8 to 18 year olds" from January 2010. Moreover, young people devote ever more time for media consumption – in 1999 this was an average of 7 hours, 29 minutes, in 2004 their media consumption had risen to 8 hours 3 minutes, now it's even more. Today massive media consumption is normal for most people. This trend goes beyond media and information consumption, but it also appears in the number of simultaneous projects carried out in organisations, the number of emails to follow up and reports to analyse. This leads to steadily increasing quantities of stored data. By 2020 (according to the IDC agency data) the world will be storing up to 35 zettabytes of data, which is equivalent to 35 billion terabytes, an increase by a factor of 44 compared to their stock in 2009. At the same time new tools of data analysis are being developed, which finds its expression in the new phenomenon of Big Data.

"(…) *this revolution in measurement, starting with the switch from analog to digital data, is as profound as, say, the development of the microscope and what it did for biology and medicine. It's not just big data in the sense that we have lots of data. You can also think of it as "nano" data, in the sense that we have very, very fine-grained data—an ability to measure things much more precisely than in the past. You can learn about the preferences of an individual customer and personalize your offerings for that particular customer.*" (Chui and Comes, 2011)

Dispersion. Thanks to the web, information is available in many places at the same time. The web has globally compressed time and space and has harnessed them for the individual expectations of each user. The decentralisation of knowledge and information sets implies that no one is the gatekeeper or owner of all available knowledge, thus no one can wield power – power is becoming scattered or dispersed. Everyone is starting to wield power in a limited scope. Furthermore, in the global economy with a global labour market, jobs 'migrate' to the place where they can be most efficiently performed, which is the definition of offshoring, or people migrate to where these jobs are located (Rybiński, 2006). This spawns competition for the most creative minds on the planet – a phenomenon facilitated by near-universal English language skills in developed countries. Dispersion is present not only in the web, but also in national economies. The global economic centre of gravity is constantly shifting towards Asia (China, India, Indonesia) – exactly where new jobs are being created. The report of the Center for American Progress and the Center for the Next Generation titled „The Competition that Really Matters" finds a similar trend in education. A growing number of Asians graduate from tertiary education – as recently as 2000, 23.8% university graduates came from the US, while in 2010 this number dropped to 20.6%, with forecasts for 2020 indicating a further decrease to approximately 17.8%. Simultaneously there is unprecedented educational growth in China and India – in 2000 the global percentage of university graduates coming from these countries was 9% and 6.5% respectively, rose to its 2010 levels of 11.1% and 7.1%, and by 2020 should achieve 13.4% and 7.7%. China is already the world leader in educating PhD students. According to calculations from the article „PhD Factory" published in Nature, the annual number of newly-minted Chinese doctors is currently well over 50,000. Dispersion is a built-in feature of Web 2.0:

„*Web 2.0 is a decentralised 'architecture', relying on distributed content, applications and computers rather than a centralised system that is controlled by managers or IT departments. This makes internal control and policing difficult and a problem for organisations.*" (Martin, Reddington and Kneafsey, 2007)

Accessibility. On the internet time passes more rapidly and life never stops. This has its implications – the digital world is awake 24 hours a day. Information is instantly updated, and users accustomed to this abundance start to demand more – if they don't instantly find the information they'd like they go to the next website from their search query. Thus accessibility enhances competition. It's worth remembering the N=1 and R=G concept created by C.K. Prahalad and M.S. Krishnan (2008), which is the underlying mechanism of the example presented above. N=1 is the individual, or client – one and only, unique, who requires an individual approach. R=G equals resources (R), or rather resource access, and not resource ownership. This access is global (G), because resource suppliers can, in the era of globalisation, come from any part of the world. These resources can also be configured in a way which is dynamically changed. This is the exact opposite of the business model of the Ford T, where clients were treated as an undifferentiated and non-individualised mass (one product for all), while all resources were owned by the company. Individualised clients and access to global resources is the direct consequence of accessibility. Moreover, accessibility has yet another dimension:

"Web 2.0 has come about because of a spirit of openness as developers and companies increasingly provide open access to their content and applications. Good examples include the emergence of open source course material and management texts (…), encyclopaedias such as Wikipedia and web browsers such as Firefox." (Martin, Reddington and Kneafsey, 2007)

Democratisation. Users have ceased to be passive and anonymous audiences. They've gained a digital identity (be it through blogs or creating a profile on a social network site) and their influence can't be ignored. By sharing information on the internet we agree to indiscriminate judgement of its content by users who read it. Users take part in what might be described as a beauty contest, where content is ordered and featured on Web 2.0 services. This content may be deemed interesting (by sharing and recommending it on Digg, Del.icio.us, Facebook, GooglePlus, LinkedIn and thus increasing the content's popularity), or they may ignore it. In

Web 2.0 every vote counts. The culture of participation means that members of a given social group actively take part in the process of mass communication. Today the traditional division between information sender and receiver is dead. Anyone can be both the author and target of information. Access to new technologies and taking part in creating the digital world become the preconditions of belonging to the web society and foster new divisions of web-based social groups: the "consumtariat" and the "netocracy". Every vote or voice is equally important-- the vote and opinion of a wise person is counted the same way that a vote of an average user would. Users receive tools with which they can influence others, governments, and corporations:

"The paradox of user control, in fact, becomes that of the illusion of choice within which the user is offered up for a form of soft domination. Thus not only are discourses of consumer empowerment embedded in a neo–liberal political agenda – embodied by its pillars of individualism, freedom and self–expression – the 'performative subject' produced by most existing forms of participatory real time media is arguably the ideal flexible subject position enabled by contemporary capitalism." (Palmer, 2003)

CHAPTER 3: THE WORLD OF WORK 2.0

The trends mentioned in chapter 2 greatly influence the understanding of what work actually is, how it's done and relationships between workers. Interactivity, multimediality, universality, universal accessibility, one global market – we owe all this to digital information technologies. But why would this have an effect on work? If technologies are changing our culture and our personality, surely this will also be reflected in the way we work. But first, what do we really mean by work?

The history of the world of work starts with the emergence of the first *homo sapiens* species, thus 'work', in its broadest meaning, can only be associated with mankind. Work, or labour, to take the more economic name, is a production factor –a measure of human effort needed to produce a certain good. From a less academic perspective, work is a personal and social phenomenon (Bollier, 2011: 7). For Robert Morris, Vice President of Services Research at IBM Research, it's helpful to apply systems analysis in order to define work:

"It's a beautiful, gigantic system — a 'stock-and-flow' model — that produces goods, services, fun and happiness" and: *"It's a systems model of peoples' time and behaviour as an input together with positive and negative feedback in the form of incentives that determine the productivity and*

quality of the outputs." (Bollier, 2011: 7).

Lynda Gratton, Professor of Management Practice at London Business School, claims that work is universal, but the *how*, *why*, *when* and *where* of work has never been so open to individual interpretation as now (Gratton, 2010: 16).

The transformation described in the first two chapters influenced these *how*, *why*, *when* and *where* of work, because in its essence work has been and is influenced by global changes, trade liberalisation on world markets and the technological revolution (first the Internet and then Web 2.0), which caused the borders and economic blocks to lose their fundamental meaning. The most important condition is, quite clearly, eliminating barriers to trade and the production of goods and services, as well as barriers to the flow of capital and people. These barriers have been significantly reduced, for example, in OECD or EU countries. Most of the other countries are also eliminating such barriers. The majority of these countries fall into the category of emerging markets. This is why in the world of Work 2.0 work as a global commodity has been redefined as being: well performed, cheap, quick and made in Asia.

At the start of the 1990s the whole Western world started shifting its production to Asia. Entrepreneurs increasingly looked for alternatives to difficult conditions for doing business, expensive resources, many fiscal obligation and – or maybe first and foremost – alternatives to a bureaucracy which didn't understand their problems. It was then that many companies started perceiving countries such as India, China or Indonesia as the location for their investment or outsourcing, mainly due to the low labour costs. Currently contacting your Asian partners is instantaneous and doesn't involve any major problems, which wouldn't be all that obvious as recently as 20 years ago. This cooperation, in most cases, is a win-win situation. The main benefit of globalisation is the reduction of production costs, and consequently, the prices of the produced goods and services, and a better use of the globally available capital and labour resources. We can definitely link the acceleration of the globalising process at the turn of the century with technological progress in computer and telecommunication technologies and reduced transport costs. Thanks to multimedia and the global internet network access to goods and services has become much easier, and so has finding places where producing goods, extracting resources, labour costs etc. are most attractive for a potential investor. The globalisation process itself has been largely a story of economically underdeveloped or isolated countries entering the global economy. These countries include India and China. On the one hand this has caused over two billion potential consumers to join global markets – which is the greatest demand revolution of all times – and on the other hand this has opened the possibility of moving much of world production to Asian countries. Also important are the numerous economic reforms pushed through by these countries, including reducing taxes and other labour and production costs. East Asian countries – China, India, Indonesia – can't be said anymore to be at the 'frontier of civilisation', but are our 'immediate neighbours'.

As a result of globalisation the production of labour-intensive industrial goods has moved to East and South-East Asia, largely reducing the price of these goods. A side effect of globalisation has definitely been downward pressure on the wages of workers in developed countries in those industries which compete with low-wage economies. Industrial work has shifted east to Asia. What's more, often many manufacturing jobs went to China not because Chinese workers are paid less than workers in the US but because they are paid less than the cost of replacement technology. This can clearly be seen in Figure 3, which shows the type of work that has all but vanished from the West.

WORK 2.0

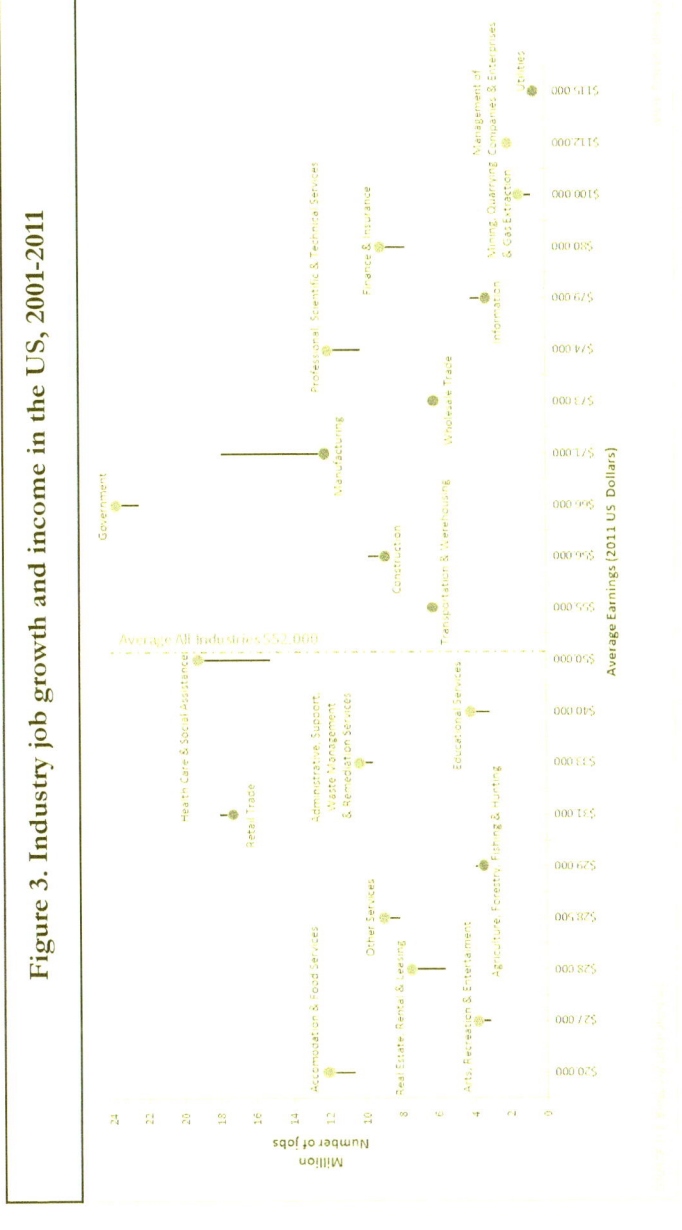

Figure 3. Industry job growth and income in the US, 2001-2011

„If your company doesn't make money in China, it probably won't make money anywhere else" – says the CEO of Nissan Motor Company, Carlos Ghosn. This is one of the many views shared by the majority of entrepreneurs. Other say that out of three items in a clothes store in Europe, at least two will be Asian-made. This isn't something unusual – after all we are completely reliant on Asian imports. The situation can be summed up simply by: they produce, we buy – yet is this because of cheaper labour and better conditions for doing business in Asia, or maybe because we have agreed to this trade for our own comfort? The 21st century will belong to Asia, as was the case always, except the last 500 years. Asian workers are working very hard to make this happen, while we consume as never before. They even win public or government tenders. In 2001 the American army ordered 618 thousand berets in China for its soldiers. This is because in China the average labour cost in industrial production amounted to approximately 80 cents per hour – ten times less than in the United States and thirty times less than in Germany! Whoever isn't moving their production (of, say, clothes) to Asian countries, simply falls out of the market.

The Chinese economy in times of globalisation, no high taxes, and Chinese transformation into the 'world's factory', focused on further industrialisation and goods export overseas to mass consumers of Chinese produce, still has massive development potential and is currently growing at 7% annually. As of 2012 Chinese industry employed about as many people as in all the types of production and industry of the West and Japan combined, while further hundreds of millions of workers are still waiting in the countryside and Inner Provinces, ready to join (for small wages) those who are already working in coastal China. This pool of labour reserves also allows China to gradually move low-labour-cost factories inland while implementing new production technologies on the coast, which would be coupled with rising labour productivity and technological development in coastal China. This is also why on 8th January 2004 Levi Strauss & Co. closed its last two remaining factories in Texas. And this was a company which held out longest against outsourcing and paid 10-12 USD per hour to its workers in the US. Two decades ago Levi Strauss & Co. had 63 factories in the US, but after seven consecutive years of sales and profit loss it was forced to shift all its production overseas, mainly to Asia. Others did the same, to mention only the clothing industry: Calvin Klein, Gap, Tommy Hilfiger, Ralph Lauren, among others. We can see the effect of the transformation on the lack of work in industrial production and growing imports from China in Figure 4. Within 22 years almost half of all industrial employment in the US was destroyed. That's 14 million jobs.

Europe is experiencing similar trends. Nokia announced in 2012 that it would reduce employment in its three factories and move phone production to Asia, where most parts suppliers are located. For example, in the past 10 years, French industrial companies, facing some of the highest labour costs in the euro zone, have shed 750 thousand jobs. Industrial production as a percentage of economic output fell to 12.6% in 2012 in France, from 20.2% in 1992. At the same time the tax take has reached 46% of GDP, the highest in the euro zone. The share of industrial production in GDP for the French, Italian and British economies is shown in Figure 5.

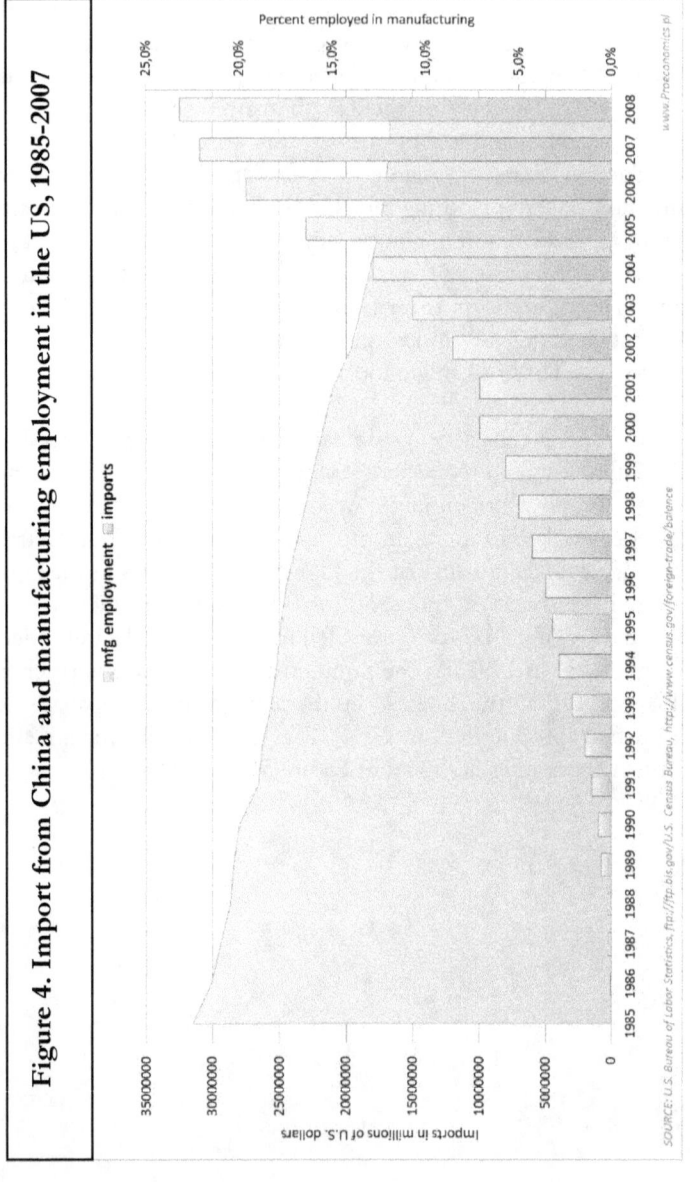

Figure 4. Import from China and manufacturing employment in the US, 1985-2007

SOURCE: U.S. Bureau of Labor Statistics, ftp://ftp.bls.gov/U.S. Census Bureau, http://www.census.gov/foreign-trade/balance

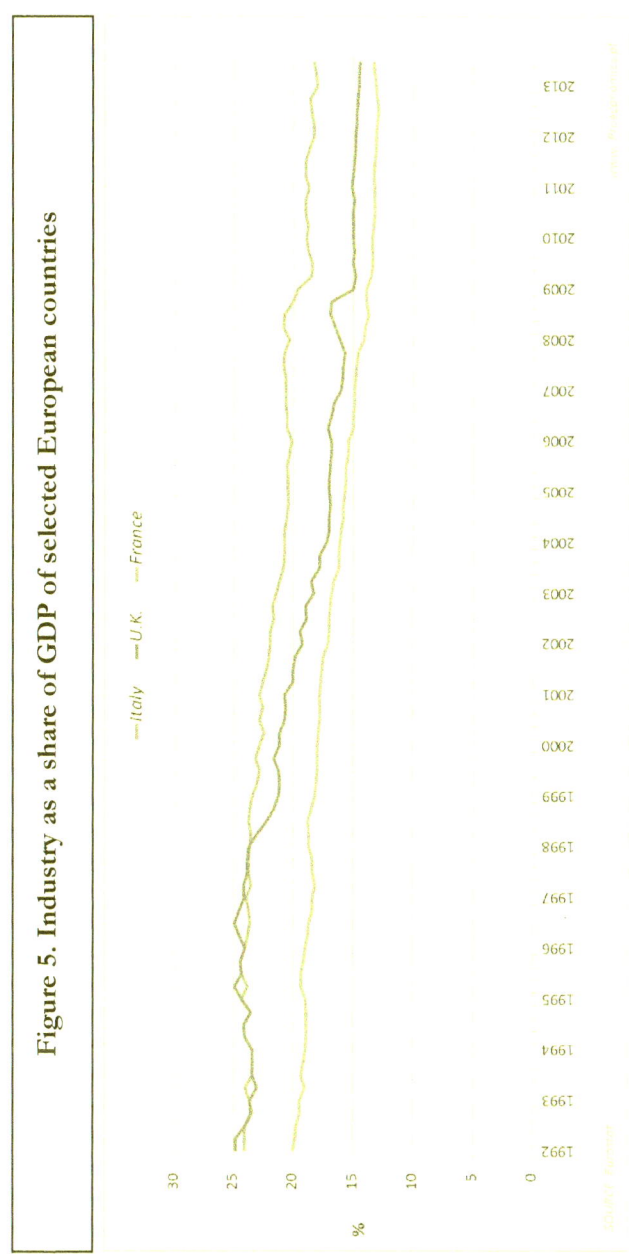

Figure 5. Industry as a share of GDP of selected European countries

—Italy —U.K. —France

In the past companies have usually used simple methods of reaching their goals, such as low labour costs. Mass production and economies of scale were one of the main driving forces of Western economies in the 20th century. The problem with this model became evident with the opening of Asian labour markets – the model had simply been exhausted. We have reached a stage of development where we either enhance an economy's competitiveness, or we stop in our development tracks. This is the case of both developed countries and those which are playing catch-up with the West. Everyone is competing with Asia, including Central and Eastern European countries (such as my native Poland), which, if they fail to continue their catch-up process at their previous speed, will fall straight into the middle-income trap. In other words, they will be condemned to always be between the rich Western world and underdeveloped economies.

Fortunately, in the world of Work 2.0 the wealth of societies isn't linked to having a large manufacturing sector. Successful ideas implemented in the market – innovations – are the driver of growth, and these ideas are born in the minds of individuals regardless of the tax burden, level of industrialisation and government policy (although all these elements influence innovativeness). Paul Romer, a New York University economist and proponent of the Endogenous Growth Theory (theory holds that investment in human capital, innovation, and knowledge are significant contributors to economic growth), has put forward a new approach to the issue of economic growth in the times of the Internet, dividing the world into two spheres: material objects and ideas. Material objects are all that surrounds us – the products in our surroundings – they are scarce resources, subject to the law of diminishing returns, which states, that costs increase with increasing inputs. Yet it is not the tangible objects which fuel economic growth – the real economic driver are the ideas and the resulting technological change. World 2.0, as opposed to the traditional world 1.0, offers unlimited possibilities – new ideas lead to new products, new markets, creating prosperity. This is great news indeed. And precisely because the West can't compete with Asian labour costs, it should focus on work based on innovation, creativity and new technologies, even more so because sooner or later Asian workers will be replaced by robots. The world of work is undergoing a true metamorphosis, whose beginning we are witnessing with our own eyes.

Today work is being updated to its version 2.0. Changes are so profound that we can say we're entering a new era of work – Work 2.0. It's a new social contract between employers and employees, where purposeful human activity of independent knowledge, creation, and conversion using digital tools, together with adapting this new knowledge to market needs, takes place without direct contact (or with very little direct contact) with the person or organisation who commission this activity. A worker who engages in Work 2.0 is only remunerated for success – i.e. delivering the product, service, and not for the actual work done measured in hours. The worker bears the costs of the equipment he uses, of the insurance taken out on the effects of his work, of continuous education, of the effects of his illness. The evolution of work can be seen in the following aspects:

Reducing communication, coordination and interactions costs. One of the organisation's barriers to growth are transaction costs. Yet thanks to technological development, distance seems to be shrinking as are the costs of travelling these distances. Today talking to a person living in Indonesia via Skype is free. Thus we can easily commission work from someone who is physically located a thousand or so kilometres away. It's also due to new technologies and globalisation that we can observe dramatically decreased costs in commissioning and implementing specific tasks. Experts from McKinsey & Co., Jacque Bughin, James Manyika, and Roger Roberts, conclude:

"Transaction costs have tumbled in this wired world, and nearly ubiquitous connectivity has made new and unexpected ties with customers, talent and suppliers not only possible, but also easy. Digitization has changed the economics of creating and distributing products, services and content across a growing number of categories. It has the potential to revolutionize business, managerial and organizational models." (Bughin, Manyika and Roberts, 2008).

The concept of transaction costs as described by Ronald Coase and Oliver Wiliamson explains, among other things, the existence of corporations. Owning proprietary resources can be cheaper than hiring them on the free market. Yet in World 2.0 transaction costs are dropping dramatically. The logic of business dynamics makes programmers send code 'overnight' to India and expect its return at the start of the next day in Europe. An increasing number of tasks and projects are performed on the supranational free market by using freelancer sites. Finding a translator of a rare language, writing a script or designing a logo has never before been so simple, both for employers and employees. This enables virtual searching for projects simultaneously with the proposed project times and remuneration. After the project has run its course the parties can exchange publically visible comments and rate the quality of the work. Popular freelancer websites such as freelancer.com and elance.com have their own rankings of freelancers, who describe themselves through very specific specialisations. Contact with freelancers is maintained over the internet, which has been described by T. Friedman in the following way:

„The Internet offers the closest thing to a perfectly competitive market in the world today." (Friedman, 2000: 81)

New technologies have profound effects in the organisation of production and labour relations, which in turn leads to changes in labour market institutions defining the shape of collective agreements and individual contracts. World 2.0 brings with it further possibilities of cost reductions, e.g. by shifting the costs to users and defying state-imposed rules of hiring labour.

The reduction of transaction costs is concurrent with increased transparency of work. Before measuring productivity was a real challenge – frequently it was completely impossible to determine. Yet today tools which measure work time and progress are revolutionising productivity - measurements both at the project and employee levels. As for the former, new tools can differentiate between worker performance, measuring who works more efficiently and generates more profits for the company. This is why in World 2.0 more productive individuals will earn more. Work transparency results in an accurate income measurement for each organisational level. Work 2.0 is introducing salary ranges to areas which formerly didn't have such concepts.

Work virtualisation. Thanks to remote working you can perform tasks in part or wholly outside the organisation, and when the internet is involved, on your home computer, at school, at an internet cafe or in any site using an internet-enabled device. Why does it pay to do so? It's the cost of communication which has changed everything. Thanks to telecommunications infrastructure (mobile and fixed-line phones, videoconferences, digital services) telecommuting is now the reality for many people, helping them to overcome traditional obstacles: distance and time. You no longer have to be chained to your desk at work. Instant messaging, cloud-based file storage, SaaS (Software as a service) solutions and other business-grade Web 2.0 social media tools allow managers to reach outside of their team or department and join forces with people across all levels, inside and outside of the organisation, and all around the globe. The pioneer of overcoming such barriers was JetBlue, which as early as 2004 allowed 700 staff from customer service to work from home.

Eighty-two percent of the companies on Fortune's 2011 100 Best Companies to Work For list offer telecommuting options (Vistage, 2011). At SAP, for example, working virtually inside and outside the company has become the norm and has been shown to create wider networks and to allow a more flexible working style. Executives use complex dialogue, decision-making and social-networking tools. At BT, virtual teamwork has been enhanced with "Telepresence", a next generation high-definition video conferencing system (Gratton, 2010: 22). However, if for some reason a company has not yet implemented remote work, you may want to turn your attention to workshifting, i.e. the possibility of working at the time of your convenience by using available resources. This reduces costs, for example, office space rents, commuting costs, and allows you to work anywhere, at any time and on any equipment you should have. Telecommuting can help businesses cut real estate costs by 20 percent and payroll by 10 percent (Vistage, 2011). According to new media expert and author of „Trust Agents: Using the Web to Build Influence, Improve Reputation, and Earn Trust", Chris Brogan, the symbol of workshifting is the growing popularity of the word 'anywhen' (anywhere and whenever). Virtualising work has led to the globalisation of the world economy, bringing developing economies to the table, initially by contributing low-cost labour, but also allowing businesses to tap into high-growth emerging markets. More recently the developing world has also become host of sustainably differentiated talent centres (Frank and Moore, 2010).

Organisations which don't use telecommuting and workshifting try to attract and retain the best workers by offering flexible work, based on a more open architecture of organising and carrying out tasks. A report by Mercer entitled „US Compensation Policies and Practices Survey" from 2012 finds that 65% of American companies offer flexible work hours and a possible work time compression during the day based on above-average productivity.

Tasks performed both by individuals and virtual teams have to be provided with access to technology, IT tools and specific rules, which enable employees to be equally productive outside the office. Work virtualisation (and workplace virtualisation technologies) can be considered a step forward from telecommuting, as today it's possible, largely owing to private cloud solutions, to create a virtual workplace, where an employee can access applications and data through any device.

What are the consequences of these shifts? In contemporary times, as was suggested earlier, a new trend is arising – cocooning. In this trend the home of a 21st-century person becomes a type of decision centre, which is efficiently managed and which can meet most needs of its tenant. Internet access facilitates participation in culture, be it through listening to internet radio, browsing the press or watching TV.

Nevertheless, not everyone is impressed with this new trend. Many people who work alone from their homes see the boundaries between their professional and private lives blurred. Not everyone can rationally manage their time. Some remotely employed people become workaholics. Their homes become virtual offices, they spend their whole days glued to their computers, sacrificing their social life or normal human bonding in the 'real world', while others still delay the tasks they have pending for as long as possible. It turns out that a lack of a natural work environment can lead to a complete lack of perspective with regard to work tasks. Such a person can't compare his work with that of others, which can lead to lower motivation and less creativity in people deprived of normal interpersonal relations.

As we've seen remote work isn't a good option for everyone. This in turn started the trend of working together, initially in cafes or bars or even in communal areas. This trend started in 2006 with the so-called Jelly Movement, brought to life by 27-year-old IT specialist Amit Gopta. One day he asked on his blog if anyone would be interested in working together. This idea was endorsed by many people. They also soon reached the conclusion that cafes or bars didn't offer the kind of space which would favour work. They started to rent shared office space, creating coworking, and these shared spaces became known as coworking centres. There's no boss in coworking spaces, which means that workers remain relaxed. What they gain is a creative work environment, additional motivation and company. Such spaces are also service centres – people help people and thus create communicating vessels. These benefits turned out to be so important that coworking has grown in popularity ever since. An interesting example of using the coworking idea is an American company, which created green coworking spaces (http://greenspacesny.com). The system is equipped with a prompting mechanism and the operating space has greatly reduced energy consumption. The office building has a beautiful rooftop garden with solar panels. Every new member of the organisation triggers planting five new trees. The company also wants to establish operations in other cities, which is ample testimony for its current success.

Different solutions and different space adaptations in the world of coworking have their pros and cons. Some like this kind of work environment, while other don't. What's important is that you have a choice – the very essence of World 2.0. Thus the most important issue for an individual is finding a space adequate for individual requirements which allows for maximum creative work. It is very often the case that small coworking offices bring together the most talented people whose names rapidly become valued on the market. Well-organised coworking spaces can provide the favourable conditions needed for creating original ideas and solutions.

The growing importance of creativity and the need for work with built-in nonroutine creative jobs. Knowledge will be the key source of comparative advantage for businesses and their employees in the 21st century. Economists are reaching the conclusion that in the long term the only sustainable source of competitive advantage is creativity – the basis for new ideas, launching new products and services, expanding knowledge into hitherto unknown dimensions (the power of creative economies). Creativity is the ability of creating something new, and a creative product has real economic value. These products include copyrights, patents, trademarks, design, making up a cluster known as the creative sector or the creative economy. They are sometimes also known as intangible industries.

In world of work 2.0 in high demand are nonroutine jobs that require more flexibility, problem-solving, and creativity what is visible on Figure 6. Calculations are based on estimations made by economists working at the Federal Reserve Bank of New York (Albanesi et al. ,2013). Note that routine jobs are those where the worker has explicit instructions and follows well-defined rules. Some of those routine jobs that don't require advanced education are in fact nonroutine, such as waiters and police officers. Many sales and other office jobs count as routine.

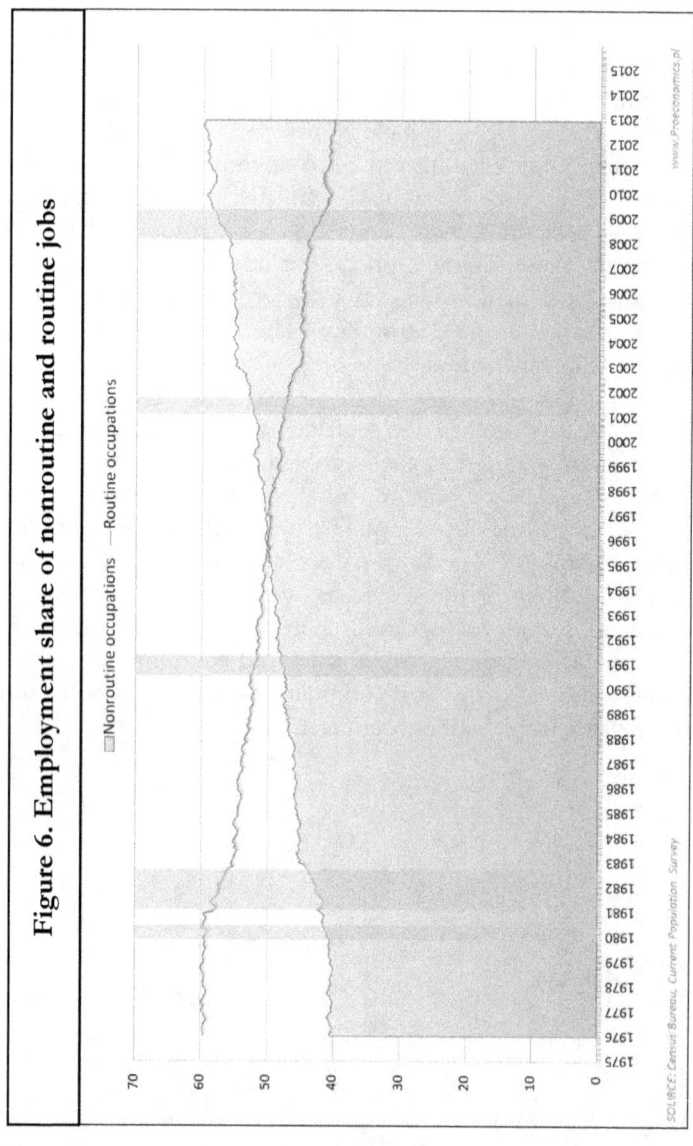

Figure 6. Employment share of nonroutine and routine jobs

Expanded creativity takes place with the rapid growth of sectors where human capital or intellectual property is the main factor of production. This is because intellectual property and the ability of creating it are becoming nearly as important as owning capital or physical goods. Creative workers with strong cognitive and entrepreneurial skills which involve abstract reasoning, problem solving, communication and collaboration, will be in demand. The major importance of the 'creative class' (a custom combination of engineers and artists – all these professions produce creativity) was proposed by R. Florida in his book „Rise of the Creative Class". He classified over a third (100-150 million) of all American workers as belonging to this class, ranking it by using the 'Creativity Index'. This group contributes over half of the country's GDP. They can be described as highly independent and flexible. These are the people responsible for creating new concepts, shaping our world and directly influencing its development (Florida, 2002). A society's creativity increases with the rise of the creative class. The best capital you could possibly have turns out to be the ability of creative thinking, as creativity and generating new ideas are key elements of economic growth. Perhaps the future does truly belong to people with a specific mindset: designers, inventors, teachers, storytellers, that is, creative right-hemisphere thinkers who are full of empathy for others. Yet creative types need to have the toys they need to play – for instance the world of web app creators is a world based on open tools; it's a world of people who freely share with each other their knowledge and their code. What's more, we should all learn to share our creativity: children at school, and adults in whatever way they can. The aim of governments in World 2.0 should thus be promoting the ideas of entrepreneurship and innovativeness, not with the help of absurd programmes, but rather, with practical creativity courses. But if we reach the conclusion that in the world of Work 2.0 there's a greater need of focusing on creativity, we have to make sure that uncertainty doesn't smother creativity – the bright and creative should be rewarded for their efforts. Creating optimal conditions for promoting creativity is an indispensable element of long-term development.

Hyperspecialisation. In recent years we've witnessed the next stages of ongoing specialisation which was already observed by Adam Smith in his description of a pin factory, which employed 10 workers, each of whom specialised in a different aspect of the work. Without the division of labour, Smith held, the factory wouldn't be able to produce 48 thousand pins a day. Specialisation leads to a significant rise in productivity, because no one would be able to physically perform all the operations involved in complex tasks, nor is anyone able to acquire and perfect the abilities needed to perform all the tasks which make up a complex operation or project. Dividing the work into increasingly small elements and assigning them to individual employees has long ago ceased to apply only in the production process, spreading to knowledge-based work, as evidenced by the article „The Age of Hyperspecialization" published in the *Harvard Business Review* by Tammy Johns, Robert J. Laubacher and Thomas W. Malone (2011). What's more, hyperspecialisation is not only used for work but also in managing personal time. We no longer peel potatoes as our grandmothers did – we rather buy a pack of French fries and prepare them in our microwave. We also increasingly eat out.

In World 2.0 an equally important fact is that the more narrow the work description for a worker in a given job, the easier it is to develop specialised equipment the worker can use to carry out his tasks. This works both ways – for tasks which require specific abilities companies seek specialists with profound knowledge in very narrow and defined areas (such as programming in a specific language). Thus hyperspecialisation increases the role played by temporary workers who have no justification to stay on permanently with a company. According to research performed by Intuit, by 2020 over 40% of Americans, around 60 million people, will work as temporary workers or freelancers. This means that the US will be well and truly called the 'freelancer nation' (it remains to be seen whether they'll be willing freelancers), and the American economy will in fact be a 'part-time economy'. Currently such work is done by approximately 25-30% of the population. This trend will force us to change the approach we take in managing ourselves and our work. For some years now we've seen increased focus on flexibility, mobility, the ability of quick adaptation to change, and willingness to participate in lifelong learning. Hyperspecialisation will only exacerbate this trend. More on this can be found in the article „Rise of the Supertemp" by Jody Greenstone Miller and Matt Miller. Furthermore, the ongoing revolution in World 2.0 is causing both high school graduates and graduates fresh out of top universities to struggle to find suitable work after finishing their education, because they lack a sufficiently narrow specialisation and no one will pay just for their diploma. That's the main reason for an increasing importance of certificates in the labour market, which certify knowledge in finance, project management, risk management or many IT fields. Holders of these certificates are ready to offer work on demand in the World 2.0. They work from project to project and are unemployed in between, because their employment is strictly linked to carrying out a certain task and ends upon completion (Carnot, 2002).

Hyperspecialisation offers both workers and organisations much higher levels of flexibility than traditional forms of employment. With the dawn of hyperspecialisation people will be able to work wherever and whenever they please. Nevertheless these same hyperspecialists will be completely oblivious to traditional tasks such as fixing the sink or cleaning a dirty carpet. Fortunately, in World 2.0 it's easy to find a specialist for all those things we can't do.

CHAPTER 4: THE ORGANISATION IN THE WORLD OF WORK 2.0

In the 20th century the employer-employee relationship was based on an exchange: the employer offered stability while the employee swore loyalty. The conviction that jobs for many years are the norm had the time to permeate our perceptions, although job contracts with Social Security perks appeared as recently as 60 years ago. During World War II the US introduced administrative control of wages which reduced the capacity of acquiring new staff. Thus Social Security and a generous retirement package became the substitute for higher wages. With the dawn of the globalisation era, stability made way for unpredictable change. Thus loyalty was also lost and the previous deal was loosened, causing workers to increasingly perceive themselves as free agents. Everyone has to worry about his own fate – this is the predominant rule of the digital world. Both companies in need of reducing costs and introducing quicker adaptation to change within the organisation, and talented workers who prize freedom, are offered a new and more attractive form of temporary work in this new world (Miller and Miller, 2012).

While both users and the media increasingly use the tools of the Web 2.0 era, companies don't always perceive this trend as something positive. This is because companies are extremely conservative and the top management (from the generation born before the revolution which brought us Google and Facebook) isn't psychologically prepared for such heresy. To a large extent companies are afraid to lose control of information about them and the possibility of shaping it – i.e. creating their image. Harvard professor Andrew McAfee asks an important question: "How to harness Web 2.0 to create Enterprise 2.0?"(McAfee, 2009)? He defines Enterprise 2.0 "as the use of emergent social software platforms within companies and their partners or customers". He uses the term "social software" to define how "people meet, connect and collaborate through computer mediated communication and form online communities". Platforms are described as "digital environments in which contributions and interactions are widely visible and persistent over time". Tools for Enterprise 2.0 don't (at least initially) require significant changes in the IT system of the company (as shown in Figure 2), there are a great deal of possibilities in terms of using solutions which were unavailable in World 1.0. Yet the real benefits will be reaped by companies which modernise the architecture of their IT systems. Such solutions are dedicated to organisations seeking a more efficient management of the company which at the same time enhances internal communication. Yet communication has drastically changed over the years.

"In the messy real world of business, people communicate, research, think, consult, negotiate and ultimately commit to the next steps that are unknowable at the outset. As new commitments are made, the process continues, often involving new participants playing new roles as the process expands. The participants usually cross organization and company boundaries: functional departments, customers, regulatory agencies, suppliers, suppliers' suppliers, design firms, market research firms, channel partners, and so on. Unlike the internal command and control within a single company, one company cannot command another company to do this

or do that." (Fingar, 2007a)

The evolution of the way work is done creates many opportunities for companies. The aspects in question are the availability of resources and knowledge and this opens the door both to task optimisation and creates space for new operating and business models. Given these conditions it is only natural that the old concept of outsourcing is acquiring a new and broader meaning. Outsourcing (outside-resource-using), or using external resources to concentrate management processes on the core goals of the company, is gaining increasing prominence due to new technology and internet use possibilities, coupled with labour cost differences around the world – the average monthly pay in various world regions differs by a factor of up to a dozen or so – that's where wage arbitrage can be employed. When making outsourcing decisions companies consider both their strategies and costs. Does direct control over a given task provide a competitive advantage to the firm? If so, this should be performed using internal resources. If not, then outsourcing is a great solution, provided that this given enterprise can manage external experts in such a way as to integrate their work with the firm's business and not be fostering potential competition. The rising tide of outsourcing is a clear trend not only in US but also in Europe (the division between Western and Eastern Europe). According to a European Commission report, in the EU already 14 percent of citizens work on fixed-term contracts.

Also new forms of outsourcing are gaining importance, such as co-sourcing, whose basic idea is work performed by company employees together with external co-operators. The idea of sourcing is also popular in its social media form. Hence the rise of crowdsourcing, a process with which an organisation (company, public institution, non-profit organisation) outsources tasks traditionally performed by employees to an unidentified and usually large group of people located all around the world (hoping for the 'wisdom of the crowds'). Over 15 million entries on Wikipedia are written and updated this way. Crowdsourcing is useful for generating ideas - Starbucks is an enthusiastic user (the My Starbucks Idea project).

"(…) true intelligence resides only in individuals, so that finding the right person—the right consultant, the right CEO—will make the difference. In a sense, the crowd is blind to its own wisdom. If there are enough people out there making predictions, a few of them are going to compile an impressive record over time. That does not mean that the record was the product of skill, nor does it mean that the record will continue into the future. Again, trying to find smart people will not lead you astray. Trying to find the smartest person will." (Surowiecki, 2005: 36)

The power of social networks can also be seen in the organisation of work around projects, with donations coming from committed users. Many of them count on the creators to start work on the fan project. Thanks to crowdfunding it's possible to organise work around a project which didn't receive funding from business. It's based on a culture of gift giving deeply rooted in many civilisations and eras. But the phenomenon doesn't have a disinterested nature. It has an element of the gift economy – according to the maxim *Do ut des* (I give so that you may give), and this creates an obligation of giving back. The stakes in this gift economy are the use of social capital created by users, as it is they who create the ties without which the business couldn't function. As there is no business without clients, there are also no clients without a functioning market.

An example of a successful intermediary between creators and users is the Kickstarter website. From 2009 over 90,000 projects of films and games were financed on this website with a total amount received from fans which amounted to more than 500 million US dollars. Hundreds or even thousands of people pull together their microinvestments to perform these projects. What do they get in return? Satisfaction and the product they expected. Drawing a comic book strip upon fans' requests, making a movie, writing a book, taking pictures or recording music, or even opening a bakery - starting a project depends on raising sufficient funds. There are many examples of books of unknown authors which raised the funds necessary for their publication. One of them is the book "The New Small" by Phil Simon, which required $4000 to be published. Within a month the author was able to raise this sum among Kickstarter users and also create his network of fans.After more than six years, the sequel of the game "Dreamfall: The Longest Journey!" will be created. The minimum amount to initiate the project was $850,000, with an intake of $900, guaranteeing a version for Mac and Linux, $1,00,000 bringing about longer locations, and a larger pool of characters, while $1,100,000 would trigger creating an interactive graphic novel recapping the story so far. With support amounting to $1,200,000 German and French versions would be created, and for $1.5 million the authors said: "With one-point-five million dollars in the bank, we can afford to bring some of those ideas, concepts, game moments and designs back to life; all of it content that our director hated to see go. This is a true Director's Cut, therefore, in every sense of the word" (RTG, 2013). The project raised $1,538,425 from fans. There is even more. Much more was raised by the game Torment: Tides of Numenera ($4,188,927), with support from 74,405 people. Other projects include a statue of Robocop in Detroit, where the author of this idea was able to raise (long before the deadline) the suggested $65,000. Everything seems to suggest that this type of work funding has further growth potential. The Crowdfunding Industry Report issued by Massolution in 2013 puts the number of crowdsourced projects started in 2012 at one million with a value of over 2.7 billion dollars. In 2013 the value of crowdsourced projects is expected to rise to 5.1 billion dollars. That's a forecast value increase of 89% (compared with an 81% increase in 2012 and 64% in 2011).

These examples show how scientific and technological progress outgrows traditional legal and organisational frameworks within which societies operate. Countries are starting to lose control over where, how and when work is done, and that of course is the only effective guarantee of tax revenue. Simultaneously formal labour market rules are becoming inadequate for the new reality – they're unable to encompass the wealth of forms of today's work tasks. Thus there are two parallel spheres existing beside each other: the sphere regulated by the strict rules of the Labour Code and the sphere of intermediate solutions. There is also an ever wider scope of the "dual labour market", with the division of the labour market between the primary and secondary markets (Doeringer and Piore, 1985). Under this concept, the former is characterised by high wages, good working conditions, stability and job security – such workers (e.g. IT professionals: programmers, project managers) easily navigate the world of Work 2.0. Secondary workers are employed in unstable and declining sectors, where there's no highly-specialised workforce and no capital resources. Therefore productivity and earnings in less-developed sectors are lower than those found in ICS. Add to that the current crisis, which has forced a part of the workforce to change the way they offer labour, and we get the full picture of the current economy. The number of involuntary part-time workers jumped after the crisis and in June 2013 it's still 3.38 million above the January 2008 employment peak, whereas full-time jobs are down 5.44 million. Changes in the scope of employment since the outbreak of the crisis are shown in Figure 7.

Figure 7: The Part-Time Economy – Cumulative Change in Jobs in the US (in millions)

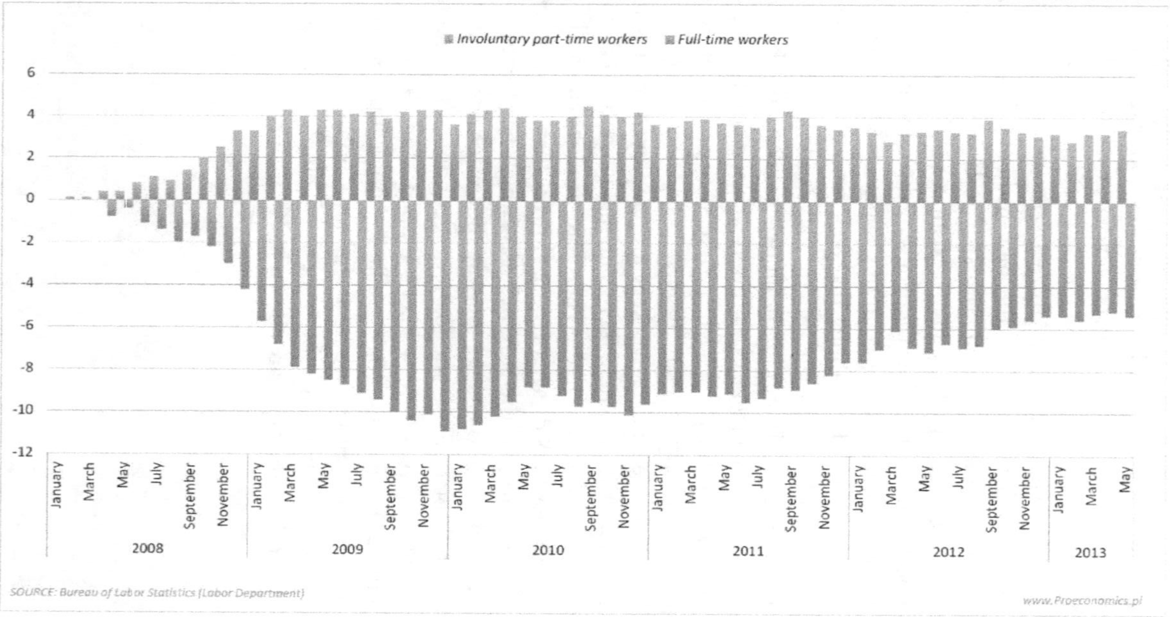

SOURCE: Bureau of Labor Statistics (Labor Department)

www.Przeconomics.pl

Currently in organisations the world over an evolution of the traditional employer-employee relation is under way. There's an increasing deformalisation of the company-worker contact. Business in the web is active 24 hours a day, 7 days a week. This, together with the trends mentioned above, has changed the way employers interact with employees. The change we are seeing is also taking place with a new generation entering the market--a generation which has lived on line nearly since birth and has used electronic, telecommunications and information technologies extensively. This generation of "digital natives", as they have been termed in 2001 by the American scholar and writer Marc Prensky, is used to the possibilities offered by new technologies and their perception of reality is based on the principles of the World 2.0. They know how to harness the possibilities given to them by new technologies.

"This is the first generation of people that work, play, think, and learn differently than their parents. They are the first generation to not be afraid of technology. It's like the air to them." (Tapscott, 2009)

Meanwhile people raised in pre-information times (the current fifty-year-olds), despite their uttermost motivation and abilities of adapting to the new reality, are merely digital émigrés. This is the setting of conflicts between generation X (35-45 of age), the generation of digital émigrés, and generation Z (less than 20 of age) and to a large extent generation Y (20-30 of age), the generations of digital natives. The latter two generations, due to their openness and education, understand the real world in a different way and demand a new approach to work – an approach based to a larger degree on positive relations and accepting multiculturalism rather than hierarchical structures, as was the norm in the past.

The next generation of creative knowledge workers has already entered the job market. These 'Millennials' came of age in a world of rapid and radical change. They are the first true digital natives. They've grown up with instant access to information through new technologies. Thus, Millennials (Generation Y) have very different expectations for the kind of work they do and the information they use. Pursuing variety in work has led Millennials to say that "needing a change" is their main reason for changing jobs. Technological progress has also changed the ways in which people actually perform work. The ability to crowdsource tasks is an example of this profound change. Since its founding in 2001, volunteer editors have written and contributed to over 19 million articles on Wikipedia in a total of 281 languages (Tierney, Cottle and Jorgensen, 2012).

Benjamin Barber points out in his book „Consumed" that new generations of Western societies are being shaped in the global culture of consumerism and informationalism (Barber, 2008). This will trigger tensions between different generations present on the labour market, both from the point of view of employers and employees. To be successful in the new world we're seeing created before our eyes, we'll need a new set of mental models. We have to change our thinking from 'command-and-control' to 'coordinate-and-cultivate'. Coordinating and cultivating aren't the opposites of commanding and controlling but they're the supersets. This means that they include the whole range of possibilities of going about management, from completely top-down and centralised to completely bottom-up and decentralised. Being an effective manager in World 2.0, you have to get rid of your centralised mentality. You have to be able to apply centralisation in a flexible way as demanded by the situation (Malone, 2004).

In World 2.0 the catchphrase "The economy stupid!" can be easily replaced by a new rule: „The people stupid!"– says B. Jensen in his 2012 book „Work 2.0: Building the Future, One Employee at a Time". Developing organisations are especially in need of talented workers:

"The new war for talent is no longer JUST about how much reward or recognition people get or how engaged they are, or even how they're treated." (Jensen, 2003)

Don Tapscott, a Canadian internet scholar and a global expert on business strategy, writes in the book titled „Grown Up Digital" about the new generation of digital natives, and how their traits can be leveraged by a company's human resources department. In line with Tapscott's reasoning we can formulate several guidelines for organisations wishing to deal with generations Y and Z (Tapscott, 2009). These are:

Firstly, work systems should be created according to eight traits of the web generation. This generation's culture and rules should be treated as a new work culture and a new model for entrepreneurship. These eight traits are 1. freedom, 2. adjusting work to their needs (customisation), 3. careful observation, 4. credibility, 5. cooperation, 6. entertainment, 7. a fast-paced environment, and 8. innovativeness. It is a small wonder that the first trait out of many exhibited by this web generation is freedom. Tapscott describes the concept of "freedom" mainly in the context of young people's job choices. Teenagers want to have the power to choose the time and place of work —a model of flexible work hours and permission of working outside the office. The web generation wants to frequently change employers, learn new things, explore their abilities with an important role played by adjusting work to individual needs. Customisation in essence means: "I'll take what you're giving me and convert it in my own way. That is: I don't want one make and size for all, I don't want to be merely a number, a statistical data point". This in turn means: I want to express myself in my own, unique way. Tapscott emphasises that this process is all about individual development paths, monitoring efficiency and a constant dialogue between the worker and the employer. Gratification, depending on the needs of the worker, can be monetary (after all everyone dreams of owning a car) or non-financial (extra time off). Customisation of the work system implies a departure from established procedures and rigid rules for behaviour in favour of constant changes and modifications. Furthermore, the organisation should be proactive and transparent in these efforts. Customisation in one aspect refers to consumer choices. Tapscott mentions that over half of the younger generation modifies the products they use to express their personality, symbolised by mobile phone wallpapers or custom-designed T-shirts. Customisation go hand in hand with sharp observation: observing changing trends, existing social norms and relations. Sharp observation skills imply a healthy dose of criticism. The web generation increasingly also realises that online they should obey the road principle of limited trust. Consumer opinions, false profiles on social networking sites, unverified information on hundreds of different types of blogs – that's our everyday life now. We're also getting used to questioning authority figures, not taking anything at face value and consulting many different information sources in order to be knowledgeable on a certain subject. So it pays to come forward and 'nourish' workers with the knowledge they seek. These can be concepts of new products or information about wages at the company. And transparency pays. In your everyday actions you should be honest and notice every worker, even the most junior intern. Creating a good work environment which encourages sharing will limit staff rotation and will increase worker motivation, ultimately boosting productivity.

Backing teamwork can offer more benefits than a hierarchical chain of command. In the past a young worker was expected to have more enthusiasm than abilities. Yet in the case of generation Y this has changed. People from this age group are smart users of tools 2.0 who can work on huge information resources. This age cohort is the best-educated generation in human history. It has unique skills in creating solutions and navigating the digital world. The ability of quick data gathering and analysing and rapid response to events is definitely a new success factor – it's even more important than experience. However, often generation Y lacks motivation, because abundance can lead to laziness. The current youth from generations Y and Z want to face challenges, but these challenges should be faced outside of any hierarchy, on a level playing field. For older workers from generation X combining work with leisure seems an absurd idea. Yet younger people see this symbiotic relation as a chance of enhancing their work satisfaction. Older colleagues simply don't understand this. They keep on saying that "there's time for work and time for relaxing". But generations Y and Z are people with an 'instant' mind – they take in everything at the same time. Their brains have gone through the interactive gaming world filter, formulating a belief that each problem has a nearly infinite number of solutions. In our everyday technological world immediacy acquires a key role – after all we live in a world of permanent availability. Everything should be here and now. It's also worth noting that people with 'instant' mindsets expect a quick recruitment process. The time elapsed between applying and informing the candidate that he's been accepted should be as short as possible. What also matters is the possibility of rapid promotions and climbing the wage ladder.

It's time to rethink authority. It's definitely worth being a good leader (coach, mentor, facilitator, enabler), but you should also understand that in some areas you will be the student, while the web generation assumes the role of professor – again according to Tapscott. The instant generation stresses diversity, sociability, creativity, fun and freedom at work, while previous generations treasured loyalty, respect for hierarchy, safety and authority. We should learn from one another – that's the most important takeaway from this message. Managing the work of the web generation shouldn't mean overseeing the work of young workers. People from generations Y or Z expect something different – a working relationship. It should be built within the organisation, not forgetting to open the door to professional success for a young person. Orders and scolding should be replaced by dialogue and cooperation. An experienced manager brings with him valuable knowledge and skills. Yet a new worker can offer him a fresh approach to a problem. Thus not always a mentor-student relationship will overlap with the employer-employee dynamic.

Another recommendation from Tapscott is rethinking the recruitment process. If we want to find talent there's no point in wasting money on press announcements. It's much better to use credible social networks. A growing number of companies look for workers online – because the internet has the biggest database of job offers and this is where a company should announce a vacancy. Young people, mainly due to web networking, have no trouble finding information about the firm and most definitely know what to think about it. The traditional linear actions: conduct recruitment, train, oversee, retain at the company, should be replaced by a new pattern: introduce, engage, cooperate and develop. This is very important and even more so given that a major change in World 2.0 is recruitment automation. The whole process of searching, acquiring and implementing workers has been modified. Firstly, recruiters start by defining the needs of the organisation in the scope of a given position. The currently used TM (Talent Management) systems allow firms to automatically create, store and aggregate information about positions at the company and recruitment needs. They enable the creation of job descriptions and the definition of the job's role in the organisations. Next, opening a recruitment process is linked to publishing an offer on websites which are intermediaries between employers and their users, facilitating the process of reaching a large number of candidates with adequate skills. As a result of the rise of these custom services job seekers don't have to wade through thousands of offers which aren't of interest to them and can only focus on the sectors and regions which are their goal. Recruiters also browse candidates' social network profiles and use databases full of applications from candidates who agreed to firms browsing their resumes. Recruitment is largely handled by ATS (Applicant Tracking System) systems, which before offered the possibility of storing candidate information and managing this data, but now they offer the option of searching for ideal candidates with minimum effort of a 'flesh and blood' HR specialist. Automation also applies to actions taken after a candidate is hired. Currently advanced onboarding systems allow companies to implement a worker into their workforce even before he physically reports for work. They enable the process of gathering physical documentation, documentation on the formalities a new hire has to fulfil in order to sign a contract, but they also offer the new hire an interactive way of getting to know the firm's structure, completing training sessions required to start work for the organisation, browsing the profiles of co-workers, or the tools with which the work will be done. Modern HR systems have facilitated a significant increase of recruiters' productivity and have brought about large time savings.

Another new consideration should be the training system and the introduction of a lifelong learning programme. Instead of relying on traditional training models, which are carried out largely outside the office, it would be worth reinforcing the training elements of work itself. Tapscott suggests encouraging workers to blog as a way to achieve such goals. If the web generation wants to combine work with entertainment and education employers should make it happen. Contrary to what many believe these goals are not mutually exclusive. So a great idea would be meetings where the management plays simulation or sports games together with generation Y or Z. This could even be table football. Encouraging blogging among workers is also worthwhile. They will learn more about and become experts on new products which are entering the market, they'll learn about their pros and cons and what is the scope of the company's activities. However this should take place using a formulated company blogging policy so workers are well aware what shouldn't be leaked outside the company.

Using Facebook and other social networks shouldn't be prohibited. A better approach is thinking how to leverage these media for the company's needs. Why? Because Facebook is needed by digital natives as much as a fish needs water. Facebook is an increasingly widely used social media that claims to be the fastest growing social networking site in the world that connects people with friends and others who work, study and live around them. People use Facebook to create online profiles or 'personalities' so that they can to keep up with friends, meet new friends (or ones they have lost touch with), upload and share photos, blog and share links, and learn more about the people they meet (Martin, Reddington and Kneafsey, 2007). Creating new barriers and prohibitions can cause more negative repercussions than allowing workers to freely browse the web. An increasing number of companies are creating their profiles on the most popular social networks. This is especially true for sectors where client recommendations are the most important factor for achieving and maintaining a leading role in the market. One example would be the prominent presence of hotels and restaurants on Facebook. The entrepreneurs behind them upload their descriptions and photos and encourage users to post opinions, remarks, and comments.

Another recommendation made by Tapscott is rethinking worker rotation. Creating long-term relations and constructing a network of alumni are very good ideas. Companies should assess which material and non-material incentives are most important in retaining the best talent at the firm. Key positions should always be staffed by specialists in a given subject and not by people who don't have much expertise in the area. A rotation model can be based on ex-workers. When a talented worker resigns, this doesn't mean he would never consider coming back. Although at this particular moment the company doesn't meet his needs, it's more than possible that in a matter of a few years it could once again be a viable option for his career. Re-entering the same river, but on new conditions, can bring benefits both to the employee and employer.

Unleashing the potential of web generation workers is a key competitive factor. Listening to young people is a good start to do just that. These guidelines apply to almost any stage of carrying out a project. Tapscott encourages empowering new and even inexperienced workers. Designing new products and services or even creating work models ultimately require teamwork and will be much more effective when all human resources are involved.

Young people from generation Y and those who are just entering the labour market (generation Z) believe that informal attire and work environment motivate workers to get more involved in what they do. If the job is meant to foster creativity, employees should be attracted by a range of amenities and services offered at the office. The workplace should be laid out in such a way that no-one has the slightest temptation of looking for another job and everyone gladly comes to work every day, choosing the office rather than a coworking space. A layout based on a huge corner office dedicated to the boss and small desks for everyone else is definitely a thing of the past. In the world of Work 2.0 the boss isn't someone special. There's no need for him to have countless amenities not enjoyed by regular workers. Great dining options, fitness facilities, laundry service, table football, gaming machines – all these are supposed to make the worker feel at home. Layout is significant as visual stimulation boosts creativity, while meeting the worker's needs should simultaneously inspire him and encourage him to create an environment of freely shared knowledge. The office design should be functional even when it's an open space concept. Such conditions foster creativity among employees.

These tips can cause profound change in an organisation.

Certainly it's not sufficient to incorporate the new elements into the old work model. Work 2.0 requires redefining the whole work ecosystem, as illustrated by the following quotation:

"To prepare for the impact and capitalize on the opportunities introduced by the future of work, enterprises must revisit their internal organizational models and cultures, their external relationship models and commitments, and the IT systems needed to connect all parties together in a productive, responsive ecosystem." (Frank and Moore, 2010)

This may also mean that the traditional model of the company, i.e. the vertically-integrated enterprise, is slowly becoming redundant – companies are becoming globalised, virtualised and flattened. The next generation of communication and collaboration technologies permits enterprises to operate in a far more interdependent way than before, thus reducing context work and freeing up resources in each of the companies involved.

Companies should also take advantage of new ways used to recruit workers. Currently employers search for ideal candidates in very different way than in the world of Work 1.0. As recently as a few years ago the press was key. It provided advertisers with the 'reach' needed (according to the particular medium) and offered a wide range of ads targeted to different candidates – from small notes informing about minor jobs to whole page ads taken out by large recruiting companies and corporations. Today, the internet has revolutionised recruitment processes. Currently everything takes place online, even job fairs take place on the internet and that's where interactions with a potential employer occur. Organisations can declare what and whom they want and what they're offering, while the candidate can get all the information he needs about a company online. Two decades ago similar actions would have been difficult, costly and prolonged. Finding information about a company, asking questions, and meeting company representatives required time and effort from both parties and physical presence. The revolution of World 2.0 has changed the effectiveness of the communication process–the pace and efficacy of company-worker or company-client relations has risen dramatically. David Meerman Scott, a marketing expert and author of „Real Time Marketing", whom I once interviewed, told me:

„*The web is especially interesting due to its immediacy. Everything is happening now, in this second. I think it's like trading securities. You won't earn any money if you think with a two-week perspective. You have to think about what's happening now, in this very moment, that is in real time. It's a big change for companies but also for people – to react immediately. Companies have gotten used to reacting to customer needs in not a very quick way – those were the old rules of marketing and PR. A client who calls the company waits to be transferred for a long time or encounters an answering machine, if he sends a letter he'll receive the answer in a couple of weeks. That's no longer possible in real time, in the time of Facebook, Twitter and other tools that we currently have. You have to answer immediately. What counts is immediacy.*"

This may require creating tools within IT systems which allow workers, contractors, freelancers and clients to provide feedback from all around the world and work on shared projects with the use of company resources. This is demonstrated by Figure 8. The world of work is changing as a result of Web 2.0. Workers aren't assessed just once a year as part of an HR process, but are becoming part of a continuous 360-degree assessment process conducted by all their co-workers. These assessments naturally occur online. Any worker should have the possibility of rating any manager influencing his work. What's more, all manager evaluations should be available to anyone in the company (e.g. on the internal intranet, where any worker could read them).

Everyone with a profile on a company social networking site can add a comment about work on current projects or

SERGIUSZ PROKURAT

tasks and assess the effectiveness with which an individual is achieving his goals. The aim of the organisation is increasingly identifying the weaknesses of individuals and conducting formal and informal repair and support actions through real-time efforts by the management. This process involves several steps: acertaining the size of the skills gap, choosing the right option of closing it and performing talent and knowledge management tasks.

Figure 8. Relationship Between people and IT Systems

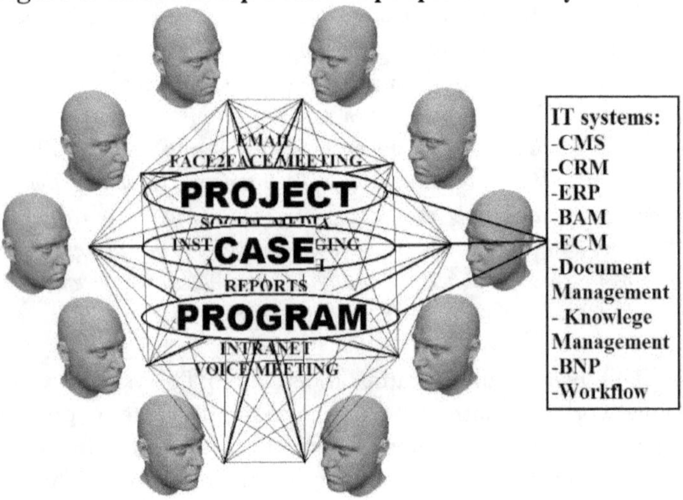

We should also mention the problems experienced by organisations which create Web 2.0. Although the companies which represent the strength of Web 2.0 are valued at astronomical figures, they often lack a stable source of income. YouTube was created in 2005, a year later it was bought by Google for 1.65 billion dollars and by 2009 had a billion users. Yet it still doesn't generate spectacular profits. Annual revenue of the website is, according to experts, in the 120 million – 500 million dollar range, and this doesn't account for operating costs. Just for 2009 the total cost of expenditure on YouTube was thought to be 710 million. The following interview shows the problem on an industry-wide scale:

„*Dmitry Stavisky, vice president of Evernote, the company which created one of the most popular time management applications, smiles while he shows slide after slide of a presentation of his company's growth. Charts cheerfully reach for the ceiling. —As recently as two years ago we employed 30 people and had three small offices. We had 11 million users. Today we have over 300 workers in nine locations. Evernote is used globally by 50 million people, in Poland a quarter of a million —he says with a twinkle in his eyes and argues that this is why his company decided to enter our market. —Within two years we grew tenfold —he adds.*
- So I guess you're making a lot of money now. What are the company's financial results? —I ask.
- Making money? No, we still aren't making any money, we're investing. For now 4-5 percent of our users have purchased paid access to applications. This might seem insufficient, but it's enough and obviously we're betting on larger numbers soon and that's when we'll be making money —the smile just doesn't leave Dmitry's face.
- Soon, so it's a matter of months?
- I'd rather say years.
- So a company which was founded five years ago, has tens of millions of clients, every 5 months or so doubles its workforce and keeps opening new offices on every continent, isn't making a profit and you still don't know when it will. Is this caused by the incompetence of Evernote management?
    - No. That's the business model of the myriad of small and large online companies." (Czubkowska, 2013)

Facebook has been saying for years that soon it will start to make serious money. Nearly ten years after its creation it has over a billion users, and has conducted its IPO, and yet financial results are a sensitive topic for its owners. While the company is making money, this isn't an impressive amount given the scale of the business. Truth be told Mark Zuckerberg hasn't been able to find a way of making a profit on the huge popularity of the world's most popular social networking site. The financial situation of Twitter is even more opaque.

Disclosed information isn't very recent –the following are financial results for 2010 and the first half of 2011 – but they give you a general idea of the state the social networking site is in. The company's revenue for the entire 2010 amounted to 28.5 million dollars, while expenditure equalled 67.8 million. That's over 39 million dollars in losses. The first half of 2011 was even worse. Although revenue increased and for the January-April period was 23.8 million dollars, expenditure skyrocketed to 49.2 million. Four months was all it took to record 25.8 million dollars of losses. Quite recently we've witnessed the bursting of the spectacular group buying bubble. As late as 2010 it seemed that group buying (or daily deals) was a visionary new sales channel, and Andrew Mason, Groupon founder, made the cover of „Forbes" magazine with this description of his company: „the fastest-growing company of all times". Until recently this statement was true. The company started with 400 clients in 2008, achieving a current total of 150 million. In the meantime Groupon made its IPO in 2011 with the astronomical valuation of up to a dozen or so billion dollars (market capitalisation of 16.5 billion USD on the first day of trading). Now it may seem that organisations offering Web 2.0 act to some extent as public utility companies, whose goal isn't making money. In this case actions should be taken to simplify to the extent possible the procedures required from entrepreneurs planning a business in the world of Web 2.0 (and not only for them). After all, in a globalised world, organisations compete with each other and each little detail is important. Perhaps „The Economist" is right to conclude the following:

„*Revolutionary new technologies require new business models—new ways of combining labour and capital to turn a profit. In order to encourage new business models, governments need to make it as easy as possible for new firms to open and succeed. That means clearing obstacles to entrepreneurship and immigration of skilled would-be entrepreneurs, improving patent laws, investing in critical infrastructure, and so on.*" (R.A., 2013)

CHAPTER 5: AN INDIVIDUAL IN THE WORLD OF WORK 2.0

How does someone navigate this complicated and technologically nuanced World 2.0? Not everyone finds it easy. Peter Fingarin, in his report entitled „Work 2.0", finds that in this thicket of information we receive we actually experience Information Overload 2.0, which prevents many people from keeping up with assimilating new data (Fingar, 2007b). Fingar points out in his analysis that office workers often spend 2 hours a day reading and sorting email they receive in their inbox. The quest for effectiveness deprives us of time for many things. The constant rush crowds out personal time and space in World 2.0 and this time can no longer be dedicated to interpersonal relations, deep thinking, or even a rational plan for our career. This issue has also been taken up by philosophers. Once, Zygmunt Bauman notes in his book „The Art of Life", a career choice was about accepting a template of sorts which was a one-off choice for one's 'life project', which then had to be fulfilled (Bauman, 2008). Yet today you have to be flexible and chase the ever-changing reality. Despite increasing possibilities of self-expression and choosing your career path we paradoxically run a greater risk of 'navigating in the mist' –organisations offer workers far less support than they did a few decades ago. Nevertheless, this is good news for the best, who can enjoy unprecedented transparency of the labour market and, in effect, a greater chance of branding themselves as an accomplished specialist, dedicated worker or expert.

Individuals unaware of the transformation will struggle in the world of Work 2.0. A time of permanent unemployment for a large part of society is approaching--a time when working will become a luxury, especially in the case of well-paid jobs. Many organisations now use contractors or agencies, and as a result these new employees make considerably less than they did before and they usually don't enjoy any benefits. That's just the shape of the new world economy.

People have less money in their pockets. Working family members who make up an average household make less in real terms than they did in 2000 as shown by Figure 9. While the US economy has recovered modestly since the financial crisis, median household income is still below its pre-2007 level. For workers this means adhering to the idea of 'more for less'! If we also factor in rising unemployment the conclusions are evident – the individual's lot isn't easy in the world of Work 2.0. This is a problem not only specific to the US but present all around the world. For example in England, real wages have fallen in 36 of the 37 months since May 2010, according to new data from June 2013. The figures suggest the average worker will have lost the equivalent of £6,660 in that period (Pickard and Rigby, 2013). In the document "Global Employment Trends 2013" the ILO points out that in the fifth year of the crisis there isn't much positive information (Ernst *et al.*, 2013). The report's findings can be summarised in one sentence – it's bad, and it's going to get worse. It is hard to disagree with these forecasts which I will try to prove below.

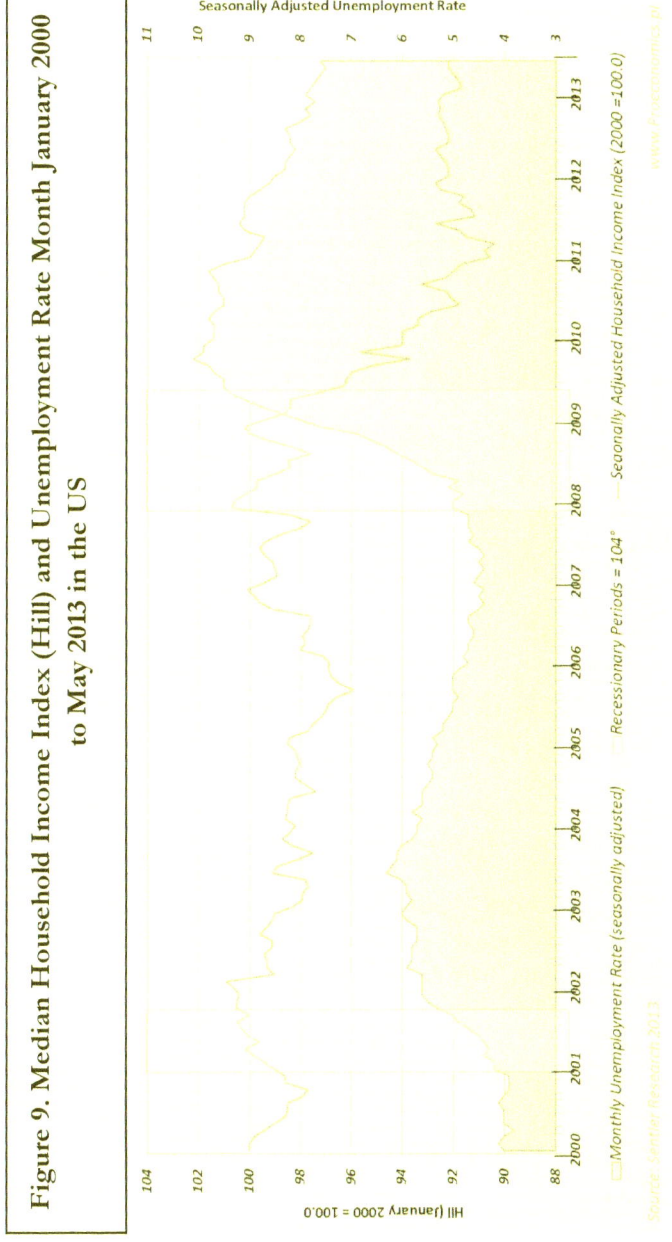

Figure 9. Median Household Income Index (Hill) and Unemployment Rate Month January 2000 to May 2013 in the US

Who can expect to find a job in the world of Work 2.0? Highly-educated and creative workers who have adapted to the new reality can. Information overflow, served in an illegible way, inadequate form, in the wrong order and at the wrong time makes navigating the web a challenge. This is something you have to know how to do. Workers possessing strong cognitive, communication, and problem-solving skills which are needed for the most sophisticated work have in fact seen low unemployment and rising wages— exactly the opposite of what has been happening to lower-skills workers. The diverging rates of high- and low-skill workers employment can be seen in all OECD countries, with the share of employed workers without an upper secondary degree declining by a third since 1995. As a result the labour market is increasingly polarised in the opportunities it offers, with strongest demand for both the highly-skilled workers and those in non-tradable, low-skill jobs, but with diminishing opportunities for everyone in between (Autor and Dorn, 2011). Jobs in OECD countries are increasingly for high-skilled workers, as seen in Figure 10.

Yet this is often not enough for recruitment companies. While companies find it hard to hire skilled workers, there are also growing pools of untapped talent. Some of these groups may be difficult for the employers to reach, but other groups represent important opportunities for driving growth and bridging the skill gap. In 2011 26 percent of employers in Europe said they had difficulties filling jobs due to lack of qualified talent, particularly technicians and engineers. Meanwhile as many as 80 percent of Japanese companies referenced the same problem (Manpower Group, 2011).

The group hardest hit by the crisis are young people. Widespread youth unemployment presents a daunting challenge. If ILO forecasts hold true, next year will see another increase in youth unemployment. The youth of the Middle East, North Africa and crisis-ridden EU countries have the bleakest prospects.

Figure 10. Educational Attainment of Employed Workers in OECD Countries (100% = total employed)

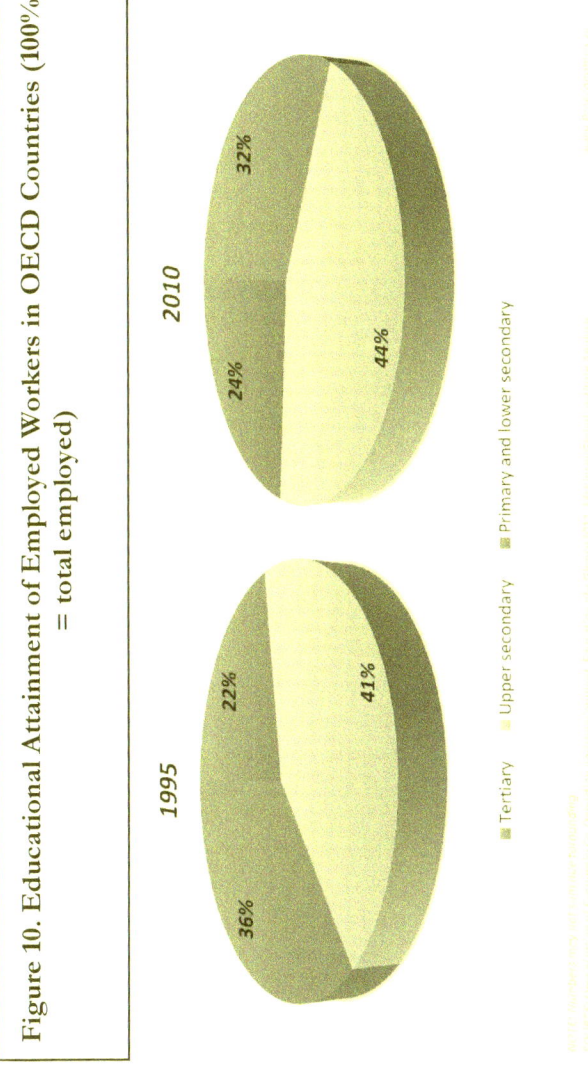

1995

36%

22%

41%

2010

24%

32%

44%

■ Tertiary   ■ Upper secondary   ■ Primary and lower secondary

73

In developed economies, unemployment among young people peaked at nearly 18 percent in 2010, and reached much higher levels in Spain, Greece, Portugal, Ireland, and even Sweden. This is caused by a shortage of highly-skilled workers and an oversupply of low-skilled employees, according to the findings of the McKinsey Global Institute (Dobbs *et al.*). Nowhere is this skills mismatch more apparent than in the case of youth (un)employment, where in many developing and developed countries large proportions of the young population suffer from endemic joblessness, while in other countries there is an oversupply of skilled workers, which leads to employment below one's educational and skill level – this is most often the case of workers who are currently under 24. This situation persists largely due to the low global mobility of labour. World Bank data show that only 3% of the world population now lives in a country where they were not born, while 30% of global output is sold in countries where it was not produced (Milanovic, 2012). And as young people are the most likely group to move to another country, the restrictions on free labour flows hit them the hardest and at times make them captive participants in national labour markets. These labour market failures on a global scale mean that, according to the calculations of "The Economist", 290 million 15 to 24-year-olds, or a quarter of the youth on the planet, are neither working, studying or training for a job (NEETs) (The Economist, 2013). These trends are easily discernable from Figure 11. And it *will* get worse. The rate of global youth joblessness is expected to rise from 12.4% to 12.8% by 2018 (Sparreboom *et al.*, 2013). NEETs are often called 'Generation P'. The name refers to the increasingly popular term 'precariat', used to describe the situation of young people on the labour market. Its creator, professor Guy Standing, coined this term by merging 'precarious' with the word 'proletariat' and, as it turns out, ideally described the situation of the twenty-somethings who have largely languished in unpaid intern or temporary work. They share uncertainty about future

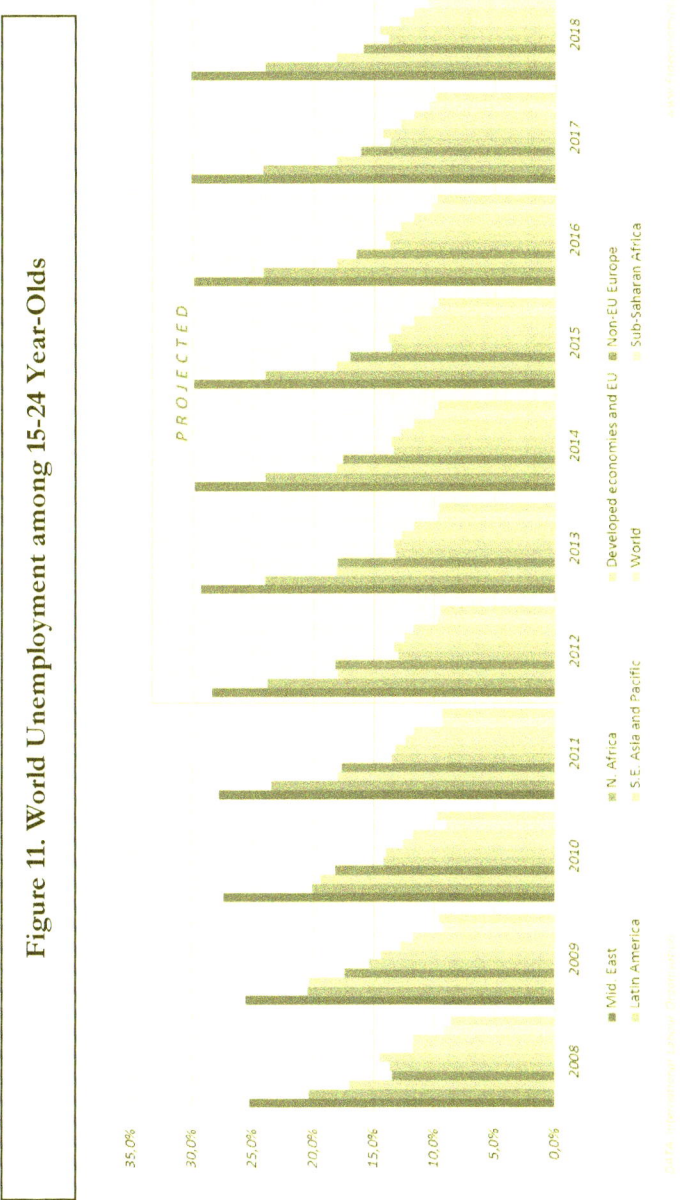

Figure 11. World Unemployment among 15-24 Year-Olds

prospects, which makes it impossible to plan anything, and a wage too low to guarantee a dignified life. *Precarius* in Latin means „relying on supplication, mercy", and a member of the precariat is considered by contemporary sociology to be a person suspended between prosperity and poverty, lacking financial security and in constant danger of falling down the social ladder. On top of the above the current youth is losing faith in formal education. A university degree, once the foundation of a stable lifelong career, no longer guarantees job security, while young high school graduates are plagued by unemployment. This trend can be observed in Figure 12. The proportion of the labour force which has been out of work for at least 15 weeks in 2010 had increased to 5.9 percent, which is by far the highest rate since the government began gathering data in 1948.

The current slowdown doesn't seem to be an exception – the highest unemployment figures are reported for young people (below 24 years) and older workers (above 50) (see Figure 12). Together these two groups constitute nearly 2/3 of the so-called 'new' unemployed generated by the crisis. If so, why are companies struggling to find talent? We will come back to this problem in Chapter 7, however, one thing is clear: the scale of the unemployment crisis differs depending on location, which also has a bearing on the political response to the crisis and its link to the financial crisis. Yet there is one common factor – unemployment is gradually replacing finance as the main problem of the *financial* system. The American labour market is experiencing the worst slump since the end of the Second World War. The number of people holding down jobs has fallen below 60% (Figure 13). The situation is improving very slowly and it is still too early to tell when the pre-crisis level will be achieved.

Figure 12. Unemployment Rates for Ages 16-24 Not Enrolled in School (12-month moving average)

Figure 13. Share of Adults with Jobs in the US (in %)

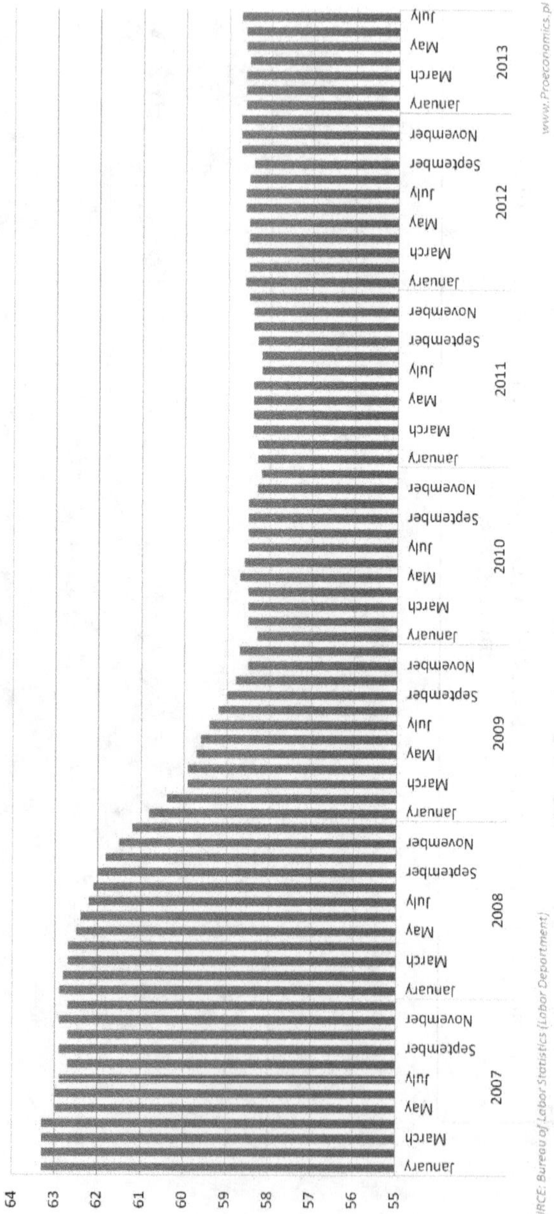

SOURCE: Bureau of Labor Statistics (Labor Department)

The current economic slowdown is primarily a challenge for workers. But a crisis is also a time for positive change for individuals. "The Chinese use two brush strokes to write the word 'crisis.'" John F. Kennedy claimed, "One brush stroke stands for danger; the other for opportunity. In a crisis, be aware of the danger--but recognize the opportunity." Change, which will allow individuals to shift from passive job searching in the 1.0 version to active job searching and creating in the world of Work 2.0, completing their evolution into a new category of worker-prosumer. This new economic unit is an individual and autonomous unit of production, consumption and entrepreneurship. The quicker this shift happens, the better.

Not long ago finding the job of your dreams was as easy as compiling an impressive CV and demonstrate above-average skills and experience. Job searching roughly followed these lines: the worker looked for offers, using all possible media and hoping that he can find a job offer fully corresponding to his skills. The candidate searched, walked from office to office, asked, etc. Meanwhile the employer was the passive party –he only placed the ad or passed on the information and waited for feedback. This is a general description of the worker's market – a market where job seekers are the most active agents. What were the main benefits of this market? These benefits accrued mainly to the employer, who didn't have to court workers. Doubtless there was much less activity involved in looking for a worker. However the two main disadvantages of this market were: usually it wasn't the person with the best qualifications who received the job and job seekers wasted a lot of time while looking for work rather than using this time for acquiring new abilities and improving their existing skill set. Today, as we've entered the era of social media, a correct application, and even a successful interview, may not be enough to land the job. This is because Work 2.0 is a transparent world – no one takes your word for anything anymore. You have to show off your portfolio – what you've achieved in life, how did you work, your references and contacts – and the employer will decide whether he wants to hire you or not –this is how modern interactions between job candidates and employers work. An employer, when he hires a worker, doesn't only hire his abilities, but also his aspirations, interpersonal skills, creativity and independent nature when carrying out the tasks he's responsible for. While experience and skills and can be easily verified by checking a worker's portfolio and references, getting to know his personality traits is often a matter of time.

Today the internet gives us nearly infinite possibilities of configuring and creating our identity online. People willingly use these possibilities as we all adopt certain masks and play many roles in our lives – we're not only mothers, fathers, daughters, uncles, but also doctors, firemen, taxi drivers, bosses, workers or finally women or men. The web brings people together and enables you to discuss different subjects, meet new people or look for love. In the real world people flock to groups held together by common interests, the same place of residence, common problems, hobbies or work. A community enables an individual to express himself, form friendships, ask questions, or share his thoughts. Thus it is hardly surprising that belonging to a certain group makes it easier to find work. It's quite possible that using the chain of 'your friends' friends' you reach the right person, true to the rule that who you are is not as important as who you know (and who knows you). The virtual world is no different and in this world individuals form e-communities. This can take the form of a closed community organised around an internet forum, or an open community organised around, say, Wikipedia or open source programming. Internet communities can be focused on business interests, on discussion, or can form around worldviews (political, economic, and social), around exchanging contacts, or files, or around websites. Regardless of profession, job, or skills, gain in the eyes of the community has always been associated with prestige, relationships with people and work. In this respect Work 2.0 is no different. The only difference is that the communities are digital and you have to know how to enter them.

   In the world of Work 2.0 the most important element is creating your image – a role which will make us the ideal candidate for the type of work we're looking for. We have to learn how to: search for and initiate relationships, share information with others, share photos and video, communicate instantly, consume information from trusted sources, participate and co-create culture, search for work or simply maintain our image on Web 2.0. Thomas Friedman calls this the 'big cleaning'– we really have to rethink many things and understand them in a new way. This task ahead of individuals is based on reputation-building in order to create positive and long-term relationships with your surroundings and induce trust. This is because the numbers are unrelenting,—-an increasing share of HR professionals looks for job candidates through social networks –and not just through their professional networks. This implies that everything you might write on your profile can be used against you or be to your advantage, if you think through what you share. Creating your brand and promoting your 'face' is best done on portals for professionals such as LinkedIn. In World 2.0 this formula enables you to create your virtual identity – carving out your own space in the global web and presenting your pros, abilities, expectations and desires. Social media facilitate information exchange between people which otherwise would probably not have met, not only because of different places of residence, but also due to different education, interests, financial status, work environment and age. Thanks to authentic engagement in communities increasingly the phrase „we would like to work with you" comes from an organisation and is directed at a specific candidate. We publicly construct and exhibit our credentials and experience. All this we have to do because in the world of Work 2.0 exposure and visibility online is highly profitable. Trust is becoming the new currency of our time.

Don Peppers, whose book „Extreme Trust" shows how important trust is in the world of new technologies, told me in an interview:

„The more we have in common, the more trust we require. Trust increases the effectiveness of relations."

Reputation is the only thing we really have – losing it is usually the beginning of the end. This calls for careful brand building, also through presenting a coherent image in all the channels you communicate through. Data should be up to date (photos, personal data, recent employers) on professional websites such as LinkedIn or 'entertainment' networks – this will help people who might be interested in your person to be sure that not only did they receive the most useful data about you, but also that you actively manage your brand online.

Another goal of a mindful individual in social networks should be networking itself. The greater network intelligence one has the better this person is suited to create innovation. The book "The Start-up of You" claims that success in professional life depends both on individual abilities and the capacity of your contacts' network to enhance them. The strength of an individual rises thanks to an efficiently constructed network (as the strength of the company increases with the network of its workers' contacts) (Hoffman and Casnocha, 2012). The number of friends on Facebook, Xing, Spoke.com or other social networks is not necessarily a measure of actual integration into a social community. It is, however, an indication of what is important and will count tomorrow: a good career network, but also a network for personal interaction with many different people having diverse views and perspectives. In the future, anchoring and positioning in an environment where the workplace is often only temporary and fleeting will be increasingly important (Ajilon Professionals, 2010).

A candidate's image on the internet is mainly formed by his activity on social networks. The era of Work 2.0 is an era of interaction, exchanging opinions and dialogue. Increasing popularity of communicating online gives employers additional and valuable tools to find the ideal worker. In fact employers are increasingly browsing social media. Mindful management of your online image is, among many things, being aware of the opinions you voice – about the world, people, but also about your past and current employer. The conditions of the contemporary labour market are forcing us to broaden our set of skills, knowledge and experience – an increasing importance is attached to prior experience, internships, training, certificates acquired, etc. What has relatively lost its importance is education – today even a person who is a graduate of an elite faculty at one of the best universities doesn't necessarily constitute the ideal candidate. Job seekers strive to show how active they have been also outside their formal education and work – thus showing they could be a very valuable resource for a company. They also pass exams and acquire certificates in specialist areas to assure the employer that they're the right person for the job. As far as universities are concerned, they are finding it hard to shift to such innovative thinking as required in the digital age. The knowledge they pass on is perceived by the market as basic and theoretical. Often their professors are digital émigrés, thereby they are behind the learning curve of the huge changes which have taken place in the last decade. Moreover, a university education is expensive and there are an increasing number of alternatives. One example could be coursera.org, a website offering free lectures from various universities around the world. EdXoffers access to online lectures at MIT and Harvard. This educational technology is better known as massive open online courses (MOOCs). In essence it's a great business model, offering knowledge to any corner of the world with internet access. Unfortunately, in the long run it may lead to a re-assessment of the meaning of university.

„Top Quality teaching, stringent admissions criteria and impressive qualifications allow the world's best universities to charge mega-fees: over $50,000 for a year of undergraduate study at Harvard. Less exalted providers have boomed too, with a similar model that sells seminars, lectures, exams and a "salad days" social life in a single bundle. Now online provision is transforming higher education, giving the best universities a chance to widen their catch, opening new opportunities for the agile, and threatening doom for the laggard and mediocre." (The Economist, 2012a)

The labour market has already caught wind of this and respect for formal education certified by a university diploma is much lower than it used to be. Today an individual looking for work primarily needs experience (which often is acquired working for free as an intern), and secondarily specialist knowledge. Both these factors guarantee landing a job. Therefore often certified candidates are much more valuable for employers and ultimately win in the recruitment process, especially now, in times of economic downturn, when firms are very reluctant to hire new workers.

Let's take a look at a short version of a list of available certificates:

ACE, AME, SCE, SCCM, SCA, ACP-S, ACP-SE, ACR-S, ACP-S/2600, ACP-N, ACA, ACI, ACWA, ACWP, ACWE, ACWC, CIP, NRS I, NRS II, 3RP, MRP, SRA, CISA, CISM ,CRISC, CISSP, CCNA, CCSP, CCSPA, CCSI, MCP, CMDB, PDM, SDA, SDM, OBASHI, ITIL, PRINCE2,MOR,P3O, AGILE, PMP, MSP, MOV, MOP, LeanIT, ISO/IEC 20000, ACT, CCP, SOACP, ACMA, AWMP, ACSP, ACMP, ACCP, ACDX, ACMX, ACA, ACIS, ACSS, APDS, APDS, APSS, ISTQB-BCS, BCS MTP, RCDD, RITP, ESS, RTPM, DCDC, NTS, OSP, WD, ITS, BCCPA, BCCPP, BCCWA, BCCWP, BCCPSE, BCCPSA, BCCPSP, BASCS, BACNS, BADCS, BAFCoES, BAFS, BAIS, BATSS, BACAS, BAWS, BAEFS, BCAF, BCEFE, BCFA, BCFD, BCFP, BCFCoEP, BCLE,

BCLP, BCND, BCNE, BCNP, BCEFP, BCSPNE, BDA, BSDP, CLA, CLP, CLS, CPA, CPP, CPS, CCEE, CCMA, CCEPE, CCEPA, CCDP, CE-A, CE-P, CE-C, CE-E, OC-A, OC-P, OC-C, OC-E, CCNP, CCIE, CCAr, CCDE, CCAI, CCA, CCAA, CCEE, CCIA, CIA, CCI, VEP, CCSK, CCP, CCDH, CCAH, CCSHB, DCEP, CDCT, CTPM, CDCEP, CDCMP, CDCDP, CASP, Comptia A+, Comptia Network+, Comptia Security+, Comptia Server+, CompTIA PDI+, CompTIA CTT+, CompTIA CDIA+, CompTIA Project+, GreenIT, ITforSales, CCS,CCE,CCA,CWTS, CWNA, CWSP, CWDP, CWAP, CWNE, DSS, DNA, DCS, DSDM, ENSA, CEH, CHFI, ECSA, ECIH, LPT, ECVP, ECCI, EDRP, ECSP, CSAD, Security 5, Network 5, Wireless 5, ECSS, CESS, CEI, CISO, eCPPT, EMCISA, EMCDSA, EMCCIS, EMCBA, EMCPA, EMCDCA, EMCCA, EMCSA, EMCTA, EMCIE, EMCPE, EMCApD, EmCSyA, EMCTA, EMCP/T, EADA, EADP, EDDA, EDDP, EWDA, EWDP, EMDA, EMDP, EGMA, EGMP, EESDA, ESDP, EEAA, Exin Cloud Computing, ENA, ENS, ENS-W, ENS-DC, ENS-A, ECSP, ECDP, BIG-IP, FCESP, FCNSA, FCNSP, CIV P1, CVP, CSIP, COV, COV, GCiWD, DIV, CGIM, SWFM, CWFM, GISF, GSEC, GCIH, GCIA, GCFA, GSLC, GPEN, GCFW, GSNA, GCWN, GWAPT, GWEB, GREM, GAWN, GISP, G2700, GCFE, GSSP-JAVA, GCED, GLEG, GSSP-.NET, GCPM, GWEB, GXPN, GSE,GPM-b, GPM, GPM-m, EnCE, EnCEP, H3CNA,H3CNE, H3CSE, H3CSE-Security, H3CSE-Voice, H3CSE-Video, H3CSE-Storage, H3CTE, H3CIE, HP ASE, HP ASE, HP AIS, HP ASP, HP ASE, HP ATA HP Master ASE, HP ASE, HP ATP, HP Advanced Sales Certified, HP Sales Certified – Converged Cloud. Converged Management and Security, HP AIS, HP Technical Certified I, HP Technical Certified II, HCDP Carrier, HCDP Enterprise, HCIE Carrier, HCIE Carrier, HCIE Enterprise, IFC, IAC, CITA-P, CITA-M, IBM Business Analytics: Cognos, and SPSS, IBM Power Systems , IBM WebSphere , IBM Tivoli Software , IBM Service Oriented Architecture (SOA) , Certified ICAgile Professional, CBP, CSDA, CSDP, WCET, CICA, CICE, CIST,

CINA, CTS, CTS-D, CTS-I, CEPT, CASS, CSSA, CREA, CPT, CDRP, CCFE, CWSS, CWAPT, CDAE, CRM, CFPS, CSMS, IMPA A, IPMA B, IMPA C, IPMA D, CISM, CGEIT, CRISC, COBIT, CISSP-ISSMP, CISSP-ISSEP, CISSP-ISSAP, CSSLP, CAP, SSCP, CTA, SAI, OWSE, OPST, OPSE, OPSA, ICSP, IREB, ISTQB, ISEB, CAT, ISTQB, TTCN-3, QAMP, iSAQB, iNTACS, iNTCCM, iSQI, ISSECO, ISECMA, ISPMA, CPMS, JNCIA-Junos, JNCIA-E, JNCIA-FWV, JNCIA-SSL, JNCIA-IDP, JNCIA-WX, LPIC-1, LPIC-2, LIPIC-3, MECP, MEF, MCSE, MTA, MCTS, MCSA, MCSM, MCITP, MCM, MCA, MCTS, MCITP, MTCINE, MTCUME, MTCTCE, MTCWE, MTCRE, MTCNA, CPTS, CISSO, CSCE, CWSE, CDRE, CSWAE, , MDICD, MDICI, CLAD, CLD, CLA, CTD, CTA, CCVID, NCDA,NCIE-SAN, NCIE-B&R, nCP, nCA, nCE, nCM, OCUP, OCEB, OCSMP, OCRES, OSWE, OSEE, OSWP, OSCE, OSCP, OCA DBA, OCP DBA, OCM DBA, OPC MySQL, OCA, OCE, PMI-RMP, PMI-SP, PgMP, PMI-ACP, CAPM, CVE, CWNA, CAST, CSTE, CASQ, CMQA, CQSPE, CABA, CSBA, SCMP, CSFPE,OES, IBS, FCS, DMA, ESA, FCA, RWMCP, RPFCP, RAMCP, RWCP, RCP, RCT, RCSP-W , RCSA-NPM , RCSA-AD , RCSP-AD , SAP Certifications, JBCD – ESB. JBCD – Seam, JBCD – Persistence, JBCAA, RHCA, RHCSS, SAS Certificates, SCRUM, SCNS, SCNP, SCNA,Six Sigma White Belt, Six Sigma Yellow Belt, Six Sigma Black Belt, SCSE, SCSA, SCSN-E, SQSSP, SQDPA, SQSVA, TCNA, TCSA, TCLM, TIBCO Certificates, TOGAF, CIMA, ACCA, CFA, CIM, VCAP-CID, VCAP-CIA, ZCE.

That's quite a lot. If this list means nothing to you there's no need to worry. Besides, this list is incomplete – there are many certificates missing from it. Truth be told this list shouldn't be known, because the value of the certificate is only for a very specialised area. In the world of hyperspecialisation you don't have to know everything. But what should HR departments, responsible for recruitment and verifying this knowledge, have to say? Even owning one of these certificates won't help us much in deciphering the rest of the list. Nevertheless, they confirm that the worker in question possesses the required specialised knowledge. Curiously, this knowledge is far from secret. There are many blogs where it's available absolutely free. They are the portals to making a career in the world of Work 2.0

Work 2.0 implies that anyone can share their knowledge practically without any costs. As stated by the report „State of Blogosphere 2009", authored by Technocrati, bloggers are for the most part enthusiasts (72%) – they blog because they like to. 'Writing after hours' make up 14% of bloggers – they write online for the extra income and to share their knowledge. Typical company workers constitute 9% of bloggers, while company experts are 4% of the total. The goal of company blogs is acquiring new customers and sharing experiences, while almost all blogs share a common trait – when their popularity rises, over half of all bloggers aim to further develop their sites, increase the frequency of posts, and also start making money out of them (ads). A blog in the world of Work 2.0 can bring you tangible financial benefits.

To become an active creator of culture you first have to ask yourself a fundamental question –why do you want to blog? Why might you want to 'say' something? We might feel experts in a certain field and want to share our knowledge/passion. We might even want to make a name for ourselves. Or we might want our website to be something more than our business card. The large majority of internet users are passive users – they only read. Only a couple percent engages in publishing content (subscribers, commenters) and voices opinions about content or even creates content themselves (creators). If you want to deliberately build your image, you should take the step from passive information absorption to its active creation. How you will be seen in social media and the internet as a whole will depend on you alone. That's the primary reason for using a medium where you will be completely in control of what you publish. Yet, what does creating your own content give you at the end of the day? It shows that you have the right knowledge in some area and that you want to pass it on. That's quite an obvious conclusion, but there's one more, which is far more important –you show potential partners, counterparties, that you're not passive, that you act, which suggests that you might adopt a similar approach when performing your work duties.

Creating your own blog and specialising in a given area is a bit like two dogs sitting next to the computer with their paws on the keyboard. One says to the other , "Go on, write that blog about dogs, after all no-one knows you're a dog!" Because online, no one really knows that you *are* a dog. The greatest success falls to those who are authentic and to the real enthusiasts. But it isn't that simple. Howard Kurtz from the „The Washington Post" summed up a certain scandal by observing that the great thing about the internet is that even a lonely sixteen-year-old girl can become famous by publishing her thoughts. But the annoying thing is she might not be sixteen and might not be lonely (Kurtz, 2006). As you can see there are no barriers – you just have to be success-oriented and create your own world and your own truths. Today's media slice up the world into millions of personalised truths, each important and valuable, so each blog is worth reading and anyone can become a source of valuable information and an indicator of what is 'true' in the mainstream. As R. Edelman, a director of one of the major PR firms (Edelman PR), puts it:

"In this era of exploding media technologies, there is no truth except the truth you create for yourself." (Edelman, 2000)

The five most important traits of workers in World 2.0 (apart from English language and internet skills) are: First of all, know the difference between healthy scepticism of an internet article and naïveté. Second, be able to READ and THINK creatively without being told what something means. Third, know how to summarise knowledge of a SPECIFIC

KNOWLEDGE AREA quickly and decisively (i.e. possess the knowledge and know how to use it). Fourth, be able to defend a decision from counterarguments. Fifth, know how to engage with communities you are entering. That's all it takes – the rest can be learned. People who master these traits can be called the 'digerati' (derived from 'digital' and 'literati', the web's elite –technologically savvy people with something to say). These are the people companies need most and they are the people considered to have real talent in our digital age.

.

CHAPTER 6: A TIME OF CHALLENGES FOR INDIVIDUALS?

We are currently witnessing intensive economic and social changes linked to the demise of the industrial society and the creation of a knowledge-based economy (new digital economy) together with new organisational forms for human cooperation in society and between societies. To an increasingly large extent the organisational culture of an industrial society is being replaced by new cultural elements typical for an information society. So how do these epochal changes influence individuals?

Free (though still not for all) access to information is bringing about cultural changes perceivable in the behavioural changes of modern human beings in all aspects of life. These changes naturally determine the set of abilities which are required to find a job or get a promotion. But these, as mentioned before, cannot be obtained in a formal university education. The discussion on whether it is worth studying boils down to the fact **of whether there is any sense in spending money on a formal university education**. Here I don't intend to give an unambiguous answer. Hitherto money invested in education made a return both on the individual and state level. According to the newest OECD report titled „Education at a Glance 2012" the average net present value of higher education for a man in the US is about 329,552 USD, yet the real impact of education on earnings is still very much up for debate, as the effect may be real or indirect, i.e. may be directly caused by the knowledge acquired or may be caused by social effects (networking and reputation) (OECD, 2012). Nevertheless, "The Economist" finds that between 2001 and 2010 the cost of a university education soared from 23% of median annual earnings to 38%; in consequence, debt per student has doubled in the past 15 years. Two-thirds of graduates now take out loans. Those who earned bachelor's degrees in 2011 graduated with an average of $26,000 in debt (The Economist, 2012b).

Education is of endless value. But, what we see is a drastic shift in the mindset of young adults attending or planning to attend colleges and universities. In many cases, higher education has turned into a four-year vacation from responsibility and into the opportunity for 'self-discovery'. While this in itself can be positive, it is far from the main purpose of attending university, which is learning a skill set and preparing yourself for the professional world. Probably it is time we start thinking about education in a whole new perspective. Education should make a person a better human being. One thing is certain – we are becoming more educated, yet the benefits of this fact are up for discussion.

John Schmitt and Janelle Jones find in their research that the low-wage workforce is older (34.9 vs. 32.3 years old) and much better educated (20% of workers with less than a high school diploma vs. 40%) today than it was in 1979. The rise in the average age reflects a big drop in the share of low-wage workers who are teenagers (12% vs. 26%), meanwhile the representation of workers in the 25-to-34 and 35-to-64 age ranges both increased sharply, from a joint level of about 48 percent in 1979 to just over 60 percent in 2011. Yet the most epochal change has been the dramatically increasing share of low-wage workers with some college education (33.3% vs. 19.5%) and a sharp rise of even those with a full college degree (9.9% vs. 5.7%) (See Figure 14 and Figure 15) (Schmitt and Jones, 2012).

Figure 14. Low-Wage Workers in the US, by Age Group, in 1979 and 2011 (in %)

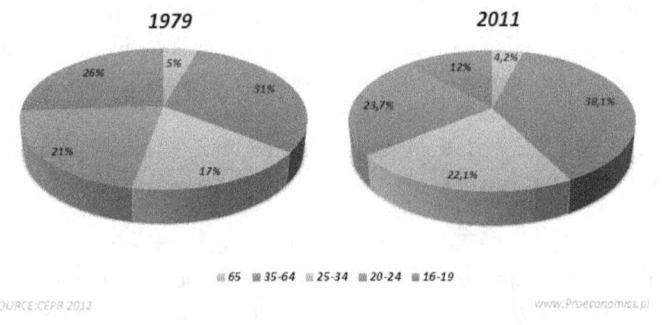

Figure 15. Low-Wage Workers in the US, by Education, in 1979 and 2011 (in %)

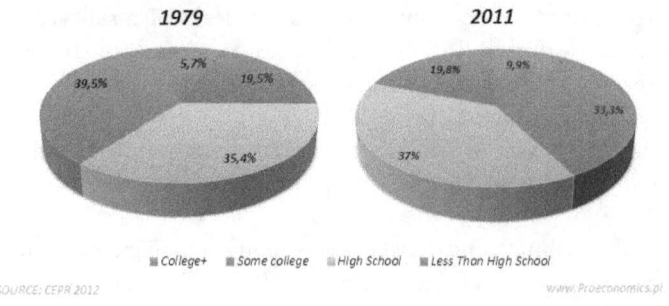

Apart from the dilemma whether studying is worthwhile (because acquiring certificates might in fact be a better solution for individuals in terms of the ROI of the time and money dedicated), in the world of Work 2.0 individuals are facing unprecedented challenges. One of the key challenges in an increasingly automated world is **keeping up with the requirement of using new tools and acquiring new skills**. Given the aging societies we are living in, a challenge in itself is adapting to constant adaptation to the requirements of the labour market. We live in very demanding times in terms of acquiring new knowledge. These tasks and the volume of information we have to absorb lead to burn out and a state of uncertainty and threat. In a groundbreaking article entitled „Managing Oneself" Peter Drucker introduced the concept of the 'second half of your life', where a person who has worked for the last 20 years is good at what he does but lacks the motivation to learn new things, lacks the awareness to take on new challenges and thus is deprived of the resulting satisfaction derived from work (2005). Knowing how the human learning process works allows us to find new incentives for development and learning. Yet adult learning occurs on a number of levels (Fitts and Posner, 1967):

Cognitive. Understanding what is required of the task, breaking the task down into a number of components and understanding the basic mechanisms of each part. This is also referred to as the 'knowledge' factor.

Associative. Integrating the parts into the whole and associating knowledge with performance.

Autonomous The stage when skills become automatic and embedded into the individual's behaviour.

Learning should go through an explorative journey, where one learns through real life action, making personal adjustments to the learned material, developing ownership and internalising new knowledge and behaviours, according to the claims of Kinal and Hypponen (2013). This is so-called Action Learning (Foy, 1972) and like other experiential learning theories postulates that an individual is required to personalise the problem through meaningful experience, reflection and implementation. Thus the right incentives are needed for people (especially those in their second half of life) to want to grow. Hertzberg says that human motivation is based on basic factors: growth, achievement, responsibility and recognition (Herzberg, 1968). In "Drive: The Surprising Truth About What Motivates Us", Dan Pink shares research from the Massachusetts Institute of Technology (MIT) which highlights some surprising findings: when tasks involve even the most rudimentary cognitive skills, a larger reward led to poorer performance. Obviously money is a motivator, but when you pay people enough, autonomy, mastery and purpose are what people really care about. Autonomy is all about self-direction and having the freedom to manage your own time and figure out how to solve problems yourself (Pink, 2009). This phenomenon occurs because people are willing to support what they help to create (Weisbrod, 2004). The model of Work 2.0 gives workers a say in a company's decision process, exhibits full willingness to cooperate, freedom to voice opinions and share experiences. The higher the level of acceptance of these values the more readily and easily a 2.0 environment can be created, according to Andrew Barron and Dirk Schneckenbergat the ESC Renne School of Business in France. Having fun and gamification are also significant elements which evoke emotions. Behavioural scientists say that in order to inject fun into work there are three psychological states which should be captured:

Meaningfulness – employees must perceive their job as worthwhile and important.

Responsibility – employees must believe that they are personally accountable for the results of their efforts.

Knowledge of results – employees must be able to determine, on a regular basis, whether the results of their efforts are satisfactory.

Internationally recognised brain researchers point out that the human brain is always learning. It continuously learns and stores the results of what inputs it receives. To be successful in the next decade, individuals will need to demonstrate foresight in navigating a rapidly shifting landscape of organisational forms and skill requirements. They will increasingly have to reassess the skills they need and quickly develop and update them. Workers in the future will need to be adaptable lifelong learners. From the individual's point of view lifelong learning is an opportunity to skilfully navigate the modern world, creatively plan your life, and keep afloat on an increasingly demanding labour market, particularly so because the next technological leaps will require us to 'forget' the knowledge which was hitherto considered a success factor. Successful management of social media today is more than a desired element. It's a positive aspect, a differentiator, because a person's authenticity is particularly prized – work is shifting from one based on workers paid as representatives of a company to a model of workers as authentic brand ambassadors.

Another challenge in the world of Work 2.0 is the **chronic lack of time and evolution of human thinking** resulting from absorbing hundreds of messages simultaneously and the omnipresence of technology in our lives. Social problems including attention deficit issues, increasingly shorter and simple statements and problems understanding longer-form text aren't just a coincidence. Why is this happening? The internet accustoms people to receiving constant stimuli. But can anyone today imagine a computer where you can only have one programme or website open at the same time? Internet language is much impoverished compared to standard language and is primarily focused on rapid communication, not necessarily in line with the guidelines of spelling and style. It's also worth noting that communicating online provides significant anonymity, which brings with it both benefits and threats, such as vulgar entries, feeling there's no responsibility for one's words and the conviction that posting offensive views online doesn't have any negative consequences. This may be spilling over to the real world.

Many people think that the new way we work is destroying interpersonal relations. That's not true. Work 2.0 doesn't atomise relationships between people but changes them, flattens and processes them according to its underlying rules – these relationships are digitised and transferred online. This is how our habits and social roles intricately constructed throughout the ages are being brought down nearly overnight. Cynthia Fuchs Epstein and Arne L. Kalleberg in their book "Fighting for Time: Shifting Boundaries of Work and Social Life" point out that today we actually work 24 hours a day and we stop thinking in the well-defined categories of 'work/life after work' or 'work/family', all this together with increasing global instability in social welfare (Epstein and Kalleberg, 2006). Due to long working hours at not easily predictable times (at night, during the weekend) we're increasingly short of time for home chores, caring for children and parents. In the world of Work 2.0 official working hours have to be only a loose convention – creativity and innovativeness at work can't be turned on and switched off at a given time. The labour movement succeeded in determining limits to work time, and professional corporations took care of strictly-defined career paths. This structure was also the context where the idea of work-life balance was born. Yet Work 2.0 shifts all the burden of maintaining a work-life balance to the individual. He has to know when to work and when to sleep. Are you a night owl and prefer working from 8 PM to 2 AM? Great – no problem. Do you want to work three straight days and then have a week off? No problem. All of that you have to organise by yourself.

For people doing physical work time off was a chance for the body to recover. Resting after routine activities which require physical exertion was equal to doing nothing. Meanwhile people employed in Work 2.0 prize physical activity which has become fashionable and necessary. To maintain the body and brain at high levels of creative and innovative thinking, and factoring in a sitting lifestyle together with long and atypical work hours, you just have to be physically active. This also helps fight obesity and cardiovascular disease. A worker 2.0 will use some time off to get on his kayak, go to the gym, swimming pool, or may even try his hand at extreme sports. All of this to keeps him in shape and simultaneously grooms his image.

The lifestyle of industrial capitalism focused on a conformist stance and discipline at work. Meanwhile Work 2.0 is a mixture of fun and work, thus the approach of manifesting your skills by showing off your financial status, formal attire (tie, suit), business look, or behaviour is becoming obsolete. In Work 2.0 we're all informal – we dress to express our personality and not for show. We express our individuality as we like, and not according to a set of defined rules.

Roles in the family are also slowly changing, shifting towards equal participation in professional life and equal sharing of household chores. We are seeing a major transformation over the last few decades in terms of the proportion of women in the workplace, which has increased in the US from 29% in 1950 to 47% in 2011 (Bureau of Labor Statistics, 2011). Women ever more frequently out-earn their spouses. This is another step towards full female emancipation, bringing with it financial and social independence. Another rapidly growing phenomenon is living alone. The bygone stereotype that a single woman after thirty is a spinster, i.e. a person whose life didn't go too well and who therefore has lower social status, is quickly becoming a thing of the past. Increasingly marrying young is what currently raises eyebrows. This positive change can be described as a changed approach to single people, including a greater understanding of them and their lifestyle.

Figure 16. Married Women Who Make More than their Husbands in US, 1960-2011 (% of all married couples)

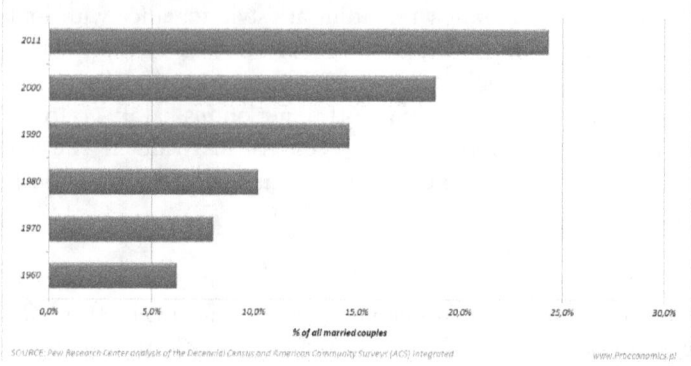

SOURCE: Pew Research Center analysis of the Decennial Census and American Community Surveys (ACS) integrated   www.Prokonomics.pl

The recent decade has also witnessed the liberalisation of traditional social ties. More non-traditional paths have opened, both professionally and personally, which means there won't be one single model of a family or basic social unit in the future.

Another challenge will be the **changing model of planning your professional life**. Career paths in World 2.0 are becoming non-linear. They no longer resemble ladders which have to be climbed over the years. When a company's structure makes it impossible to develop your career (and this is very common for companies working in the context of Work 1.0) people say: „There are no growth opportunities for me here" and simply leave. I know people who want to be a member of the board within, say, 8 years, and nothing less will satisfy them. Work 2.0 implies frequent changes of employer – from project to project, from contract to contract. Becoming part of the structure of Work 2.0 involves a larger number of employers throughout your career which we will start to assess from a project-based point of view. Change becomes more dramatic and unexpected.

Various strategies of managing time for the duration of a

lifetime are being created, among which the most popular include, according to B. Jung (2010), the following:

Front-loading – involving concentrating most of one's work over the first 10-20 years of professional life, often implying working for a dozen or so hours per day, in order to cut back on work hours after the initial period and taking time to enjoy life.

Deferred life plan – as above, but it involves postponing not only the pleasure of enjoying life, but also having children. This directly affects demographics.

Life-shifting – the upper age limit of our professional activity is shifting upwards, together with the odd gap year during the time we're active.

Time-deepening – a more effective use of our time, to the extent possible, by speeding up some activities (shorter meals, choosing a workplace according to the distance which has to be travelled, replacing your own work with that of others, introducing multitasking – doing many things at the same time.

Based on the observation of careers in the world of the web, you need an identity to find your place in the digital world. You not only have to find your place in society, as was the case before, but also have to create your own work identity, which causes us to be associated with certain projects, programmes or successfully performed tasks. A significant success factor is learning to manage your presence in social networks and learning new ways of building relationships and acquiring contacts whose importance can't be overestimated.

Finally, **the scope of freedom enjoyed by an individual is changing and consequently the effects of using this freedom are changing**. As recently as 10 years ago we were pretty sure we wouldn't become addicted to mobile phones.

Today they're the basic element of living in a modern society. Before hearing „Do some work during the weekend" was something terrible. Today this is normal. The same applies to the need of permanent internet connectivity and immediacy. Want it or not – we have to!

In his article „We think. The power of mass-creativity", Charles Leadbeater wrote about the way of boosting the collective intelligence of many users through joint efforts and wise leveraging of technology, which could lead to more democracy, promote freedom, mitigate inequality and enable collective creativity (Leadbeater, 2009). Thanks to the continually repeated positive associations with what is 'social', 'social media' have entered public awareness not only at the level of the original meaning, referring also to social organisation and interaction. To name an example, freedom of speech is a value permanently encrusted in the idea of the internet, it is in essence part of a web identity, which causes justified protests against any moves to regulate this medium. A step further from this idea is World 2.0. Specific examples of using applications from Web 2.0 – e.g. during the successful electoral campaign of president Obama in 2008 or during the so-called Green Movement in Iran in 2009 – have produced a strong belief in the liberalising potential of technology. Unlimited digital data storage, unlimited transmissions and an unregulated internet have restored people to the role of basic entities: they have been given the right to choose and the right to communicate. The web has caused a turn towards more individualism and uniqueness of any individual and his opinions -which is the very concept taken away by the mass media in the 20th century. The world in the previous century was structured in a top-down way – all decisions came from above, along a hierarchically-defined chain of command (defined by corporations, politicians, programmes). In this century the world is returning to its bottom-up state. Decentralisation, as mentioned in Chapter 2, is one of the elements of World 2.0 – this process is helped along by the universal availability of Web 2.0 tools.

Nevertheless, we should remember that the limits to freedom, including freedom of speech (and intellectual property) on the internet are, at least in theory, determined as they have been in the real world. The freedom of a person living in society is subject to many limitations, if only resulting from the norms of coexistence. Although the limits of social norms aren't usually rigid and often shift in many ways, usually motivated by expanding individual freedom, their sheer existence isn't questioned. To the contrary, they are a significant and absolutely indispensable value in the life of any society, i.e. they have global value. Thus two significant values coexist and are mutually dependent: individual freedom on the one hand, and social norms of life on the other. They evolve as best as they can. Yet it is worth noting that Web 2.0, for instance expressed by the blogosphere and generally linked to freedom of speech, can be subject to surveillance and become an element of supervising citizens. The internet offers huge opportunities for governments, companies and other institutions to spy on users, gather information and enact control. The same applies to work. Work 2.0 implies an incredible expansion in the freedom for individuals to define and coordinate their work, but this work will increasingly be subject to more and more control.

CHAPTER 7: WORK 2.0 REPERCUSSIONS. ARE MACHINES OUR BEST FRIENDS?

The personal computer changed the rules of the game in the business world. Meanwhile the internet and Web 2.0 are destroying many established social structures and business models and are leading to the evolution of the way we understand work. Like organisations which are being flattened in World 2.0, so too Work 2.0 is becoming flatter, that is, less hierarchical. It is also becoming more automated and its most significant trait is the effectiveness of work processes. Automation means that a lot of work is taken from our hands by machines.

"U.S. Labor Force Participation Rate Lowest Since 1979" – that was the title the "Huffington Post" tried to scare us with on the 6th April 2013 (Wiseman and Washington, 2013). The labour force participation rate is the percentage of working-age people in an economy who are either employed or unemployed but looking for a job. Indeed the labour force participation rate is 2.5 percentage points lower than it was at the start of the recession. So for every 10,000 people age 16 and older (excluding members of the military) 250 fewer are working or looking for a job than in December 2007 (Figure 17). But you would be fooled to think that the crisis is the reason for this. True, it may have hastened certain processes going on in the economy. But the current high unemployment in most of the world may have little to do with the current economic slowdown or the dispute between economic authorities on more market or state in economic decisions. Yes, this discussion can nudge the media back and forth in their opinions, but there are much stronger forces at work here.

In many countries real unemployment is at many times that of official numbers. This is the case in Russia, for instance, where it is 16 times higher than government data and three times that of statistical measures. Also the US, upon closer inspection, has high levels of people lacking work (Figure 17 and Figure 18). It's worth taking a look at the data: the labour force participation rate and the broadest measure of joblessness (U6). U6 includes everyone in the official unemployment rate plus marginally attached workers, who are neither working nor looking for work, it tells us that it's more and more difficult to find a job (it also includes people who want a full-time job but are working part-time instead because they couldn't find anything else).

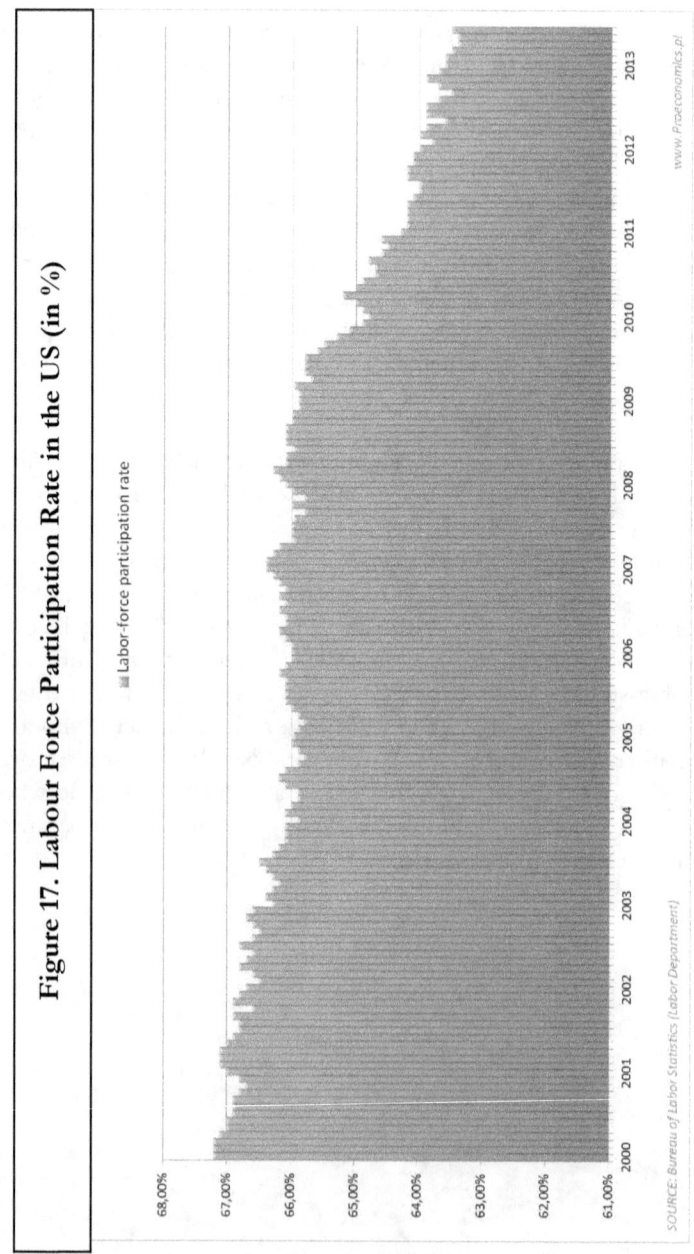

Figure 17. Labour Force Participation Rate in the US (in %)

SOURCE: Bureau of Labor Statistics (Labor Department)

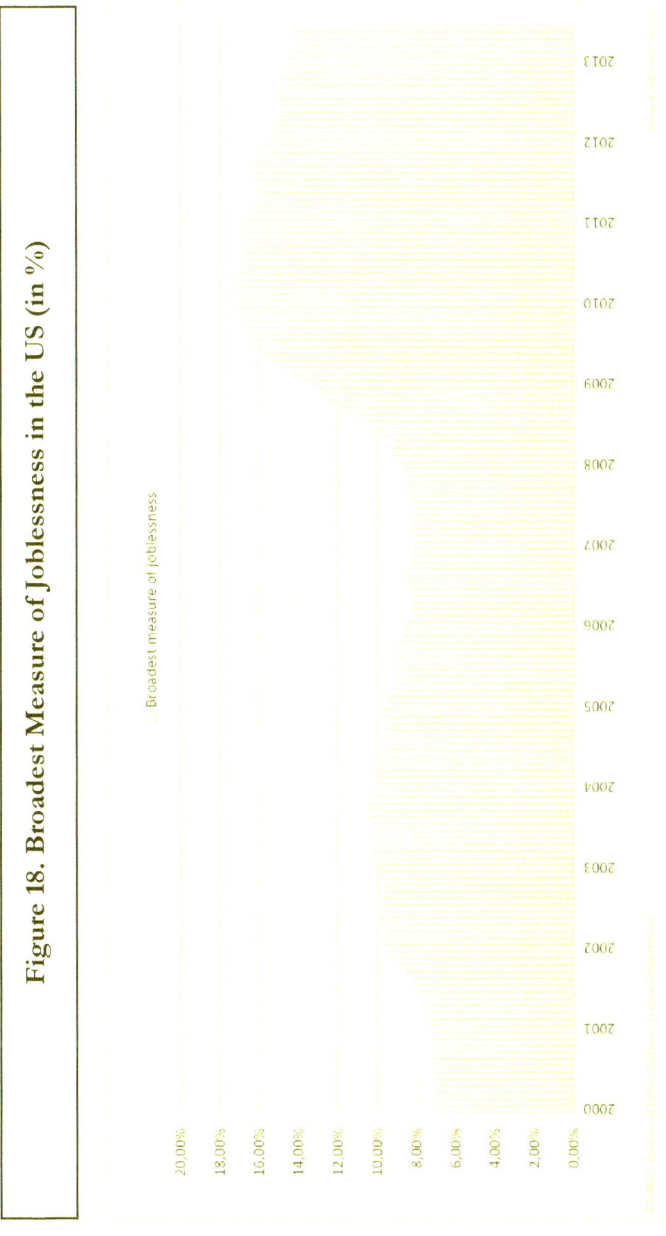

Figure 18. Broadest Measure of Joblessness in the US (in %)

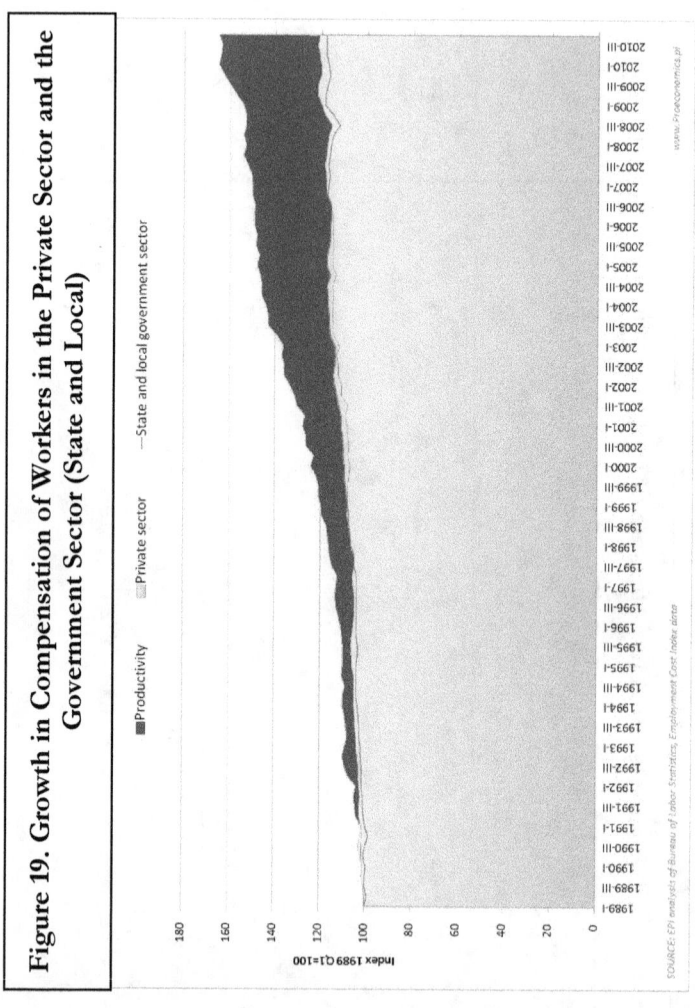

Figure 19. Growth in Compensation of Workers in the Private Sector and the Government Sector (State and Local)

We love new technology. I myself have to admit to being a geek. This new technology we have come to worship is being adopted by all kinds of organisations which employ people. It's replacing workers in large corporations and small businesses alike, in blue chip companies and start-ups too. It's being used by schools, colleges and universities, hospitals and other medical facilities are enthusiastic users too, and don't forget about non-profit organisations and the military. But every new efficiency-improving technology brings with it job destruction. That's what efficiency means – not having to pay someone the same amount as before – or not paying him at all in the case of automation. The cotton gin meant that people no longer had to pick by hand, neither do people weave by hand anymore. This is great news – it gives the economy the ability to produce more goods and services. The productivity of work increases with the adoption of new technologies. Unfortunately, in recent decades wage increases haven't risen in tandem with this rise of productivity. Workers have suffered from decades of stagnating wages despite large gains in productivity (Mishel and Shierholz, 2011). Let's take a look at Figure 19.

Why have wages not kept up with productivity? The answer is that the economy's structure is geared towards the expectations of the well off and not towards producing good jobs and improved living standards (Bivens, 2011). The significant growth in productivity, income, and wealth in the recent decades should have generated (and certainly could have generated) at least some wage hikes for American workers. Reversing the decoupling of the growth of workers' pay and productivity is a major challenge facing policymakers (Mishel and Shierholz, 2011). We will come back to this in the next part of this chapter. But first we should acknowledge that today a bigger challenge for the labour market, which despite economic growth and thus a rising GDP *per capita* in developed countries isn't generating new jobs, is automation – the automation of both physical work taken from us by machines and, increasingly so, of cognitive work.

Until recently workers driven out of factories by robots could go work somewhere else while economists were busy discrediting the arguments of Ned Ludd, the patron saint of the Luddite movement in 19th-century Britain, which held that machines were taking away work from people. Original Luddites violently opposed these machines and often broke them. Although the Industrial Revolution destroyed most work opportunities in workshops it brought a couple of new, important things to the economy: it increased efficiency, which raised wages, and it brought mechanisation as the main driver of solving many problems of civilisation. Economists believe that recent technological change has been 'skill-biased', which is to say that new technologies are substitutes for low-skilled labour or may be complementary to high-skilled labour. As for unskilled workers, routine and simple tasks can be automated. Technology may increase the demand for skills in many ways. Directly, new technologies such as IT are complicated to use and require people with a certain skill set necessary to operate them. Technology also increases skilled labour demand indirectly by introducing changes to company structure and work organisation. Information and communications technologies allow for more frequent and complex interactions within and between companies, their customers and suppliers, requiring better communication skills and the ability to assimilate information from many different sources (Bresnahan, Brynjolfsson and Hitt, 2002).

Machines don't fall ill, they are simply cheaper and less prone to error than people. Besides they're incredibly repetitive. Whether technological progress is eating up jobs is the area of interest of an increasing number of economists, somewhat traditionally called Luddites 2.0 – although they haven't taken to destroying machines just yet. Their pessimistic assumptions are that the consequences of spreading technological progress will be a sharp and uncontrollable fall of demand for labour caused by its increased effectiveness. A good example of this trend is the vision of Jeremy Rifkin, who he himself calls the 'end of work' (1996). In the information era intelligent machines will eliminate human labour from the process of producing goods and services. According to Rifkin, 75% of human labour in advanced economies is simple enough to be replaced by machines.

'Optimistic' scholars take a different approach. It's worth examining closely what they have to say. They regard globalisation to be a driving force of positive change, because it grants the possibility of obtaining an education and achieving higher income from your work. But for that to happen job seekers have to adapt. Thus there will always be a gulf between the huge demand for low-skilled labour (or jobs for anyone) and demand for highly-skilled workers, who will occupy the few managerial positions (Reich, 1992). The digital economy provides opportunities for many people - opportunities which would not exist otherwise. Self-published Kindle eBooks constitute around 30% of the bestselling Kindle books and their authors receive 70% royalties (much higher than in the case of traditional publishing) – these authors would probably never earn any money without this option. Successful blogs, many of them run by ordinary individuals, have enormous earning potential and are generally written by people who before the web revolution would never have been given a chance to shine. Artists with highly popular YouTube videos can make a lot of money by placing ads on their videos – another source of income which would not exist otherwise – together with the exposure they receive which may lead to recording contracts, which otherwise would have been impossible for them to obtain. Technology is, in fact, a good thing. Eating up jobs is a good thing because it creates efficiency and frees up people's time. Of course this means that there are fewer jobs, but profits are higher, and what's even more important is the satisfaction efficiency generates. We might be on the verge of a fantastic new era… if we ALL manage to enter into its heydays. Technology isn't at fault;

rather it's our slowness to adapt to it as a society. We still live in a 20th century economic model but have 21st century technology.

In contrast to the times of Ludd, we currently observe that a quicker transformation has left people unable to keep up and adapt their abilities, becoming unemployed in the process. In other words the pace of innovation is accelerating exponentially, following Moore's Law. Gordon Moore, co-founder of Intel, observed that the efficiency (processing power) of microprocessors is doubled every 18 months, while its production costs halves. In 1964, when Moore first announced his law, to cost of one processing unit (Floating Point Operations Per Second) was one million dollars. Currently its cost is less than one cent. Moore's formula started to play an important role in global technological development. Today we are faced with the problem that people can't accelerate their skills development or retool their purpose in life that fast. Is technology indeed destroying jobs faster than it is creating new ones?

In addition to the vast amount of time required to learn for people to learn and adapt to new skills, another downside is that , computers and the internet have caused many jobs to vanish from personal secretaries, replaced by smartphones, all the way to travel agents. Are you booking your vacation with an online app? You've helped lay off a travel agent. The same goes for journalists, who are losing jobs because all they've previously created is now available for free. There are companies offering software which can create journalistic content, for example, Automated Insights based in Durham, North Carolina, whose programmes create automated sports articles, a thousand per minute. It may not be grand journalism, but short notes with match scores can be perfectly handled by some formulas and algorithms. Next in line for the axe are call centres (due to the technology of speech synthesis) and translators (owing to increasing quality of automated translation systems). But even professionals can't feel safe – even the fate of lawyers might be in danger. John Markoff wrote in March 2011 in the „New York Times" about legions of expensive lawyers being replaced by software. The e-discovery company from Silicon Valley, Clearwell, has developed software which analyses documents and finds concepts rather than specific keywords, limiting the time required to locate relevant information in litigation. Clearwell's software searches through millions of documents and makes the court-imposed deadline of one week, identifying documents relevant to the court-ordered discovery motion. John Markoff says:

„E-discovery technologies generally fall into two broad categories that can be described as "linguistic" and "sociological." The most basic linguistic approach uses specific search words to find and sort relevant documents. More advanced programs filter documents through a large web of word and phrase definitions. A user who types "dog" will also find documents that mention "man's best friend" and even the notion of a "walk." (Markoff, 2011).

Some might say: great news! Yes to e-lawyers! Someone else might add sarcastically, "For me the advantage is that unlike 'flesh-and-blood' lawyers, computers don't devour their own young." "Lawyers usually don't have a good reputation – most people may actually be pleased. Society as a whole will gain – lawyers will lose." The US is home to more than a quarter of all lawyers in the entire world, thus some might say that lowering their numbers is a boon. But what happens if other professions follow in the footsteps of lawyers? Who will pay them? Eventually, technology will get to everybody. Few people can understand the complexity of what 'free' means in a modern world and its implications for good and bad. It's great having free content, music or video, but that's the fundamental problem right there. If you have all this for free, then you're a hobbyist, and being a hobbyist, you call this a 'privilege'. You think it's all about passion. Certainly there are many artists, musicians, writers and journalists who get huge satisfaction from what they do, but they're professionals and have spent significant time and money on training.

"*My children have been brought up in a world where they have to compete with those who will work for free. It is only a matter of time until we will all be asked to do the same. And I refuse. (…) The digital economy operates as a kind of sophisticated X Factor: someone will make it, but most won't – and the real loser is society*". (Moore, 2013)

Access to abundance – this is how the digital economy can be described. Economics traditionally has dealt with scarcity and lack of efficiency, i.e. lack of equilibrium between supply and demand. In the digital economy supply and demand lose their original meaning – nearly everything is available (because it's virtual and intangible). The economics of abundance must lead to a drop of production costs and prices. Some employees agree to work for less, or even for free, because they have less bargaining power than previous generations. A couple of decades ago business was reliant on workers – without their engagment, knowledge, and dedication there would be no profits. Yet currently companies rely more on technology than they do on human labour.

Not everyone's thrilled (artists, journalists, film producers definitely aren't). On the other hand, I doubt my readers would say no to a free article or book. And what is the real scale of job replacement we're actually talking about? Associated Press analysed employment data from 20 countries, tracked changes in hiring by industry, pay and task, compared job losses and gains during recessions and expansions over the past four decades and interviewed economists, technology experts, robot manufacturers, software developers, entrepreneurs and people in the labour force who ranged from CEOs to the unemployed. After performing this analysis and playing around with the numbers they found that in the US half of all 'disappeared' 7.5 million jobs were in sectors which pay

$38,000 - $68,000 annually – more than physical work pays. Yet although since 2009 the market 'reclaimed' 3.5 million jobs, only 2 percent went to this middle-income group. 70 percent went to lower-income groups, and 30 percent to higher paying jobs. New jobs are being created, but not the middle-paying ones. The AP finds productivity – boosted by new technology – increased thanks to these changes. For instance Gary, Indiana reduced its bus driver employment by 60 percent, as the routes were optimised using specialised software. Meanwhile the Seattle police department used special software, which generates reports directly from laptops, to send police officers back out to the field. As for the scale of the changes, companies in the S&P's 500 stock index reported profits a third higher than in the year before the Great Recession. They've also expanded their businesses' operations, while their total employment has declined by half a million to a level of 21.1 million. In the Euro area 7.6 million middle-income jobs have vanished since 2008. According to economist Maarten Goos two-thirds of these losses have been caused by technology (Goos, Manning and Salomons, 2009). "The recessions have amplified the trend," says Goos. Technology is replacing workers in the advanced economies regardless of their politics, policies and laws. Union rules and labour laws might be responsible for slowing the process down, but no country would attempt to prohibit organisations from using technology which allows them to operate in a more efficient way and with fewer employees. In the coming years the developed world may face years of high middle-class unemployment, social discord, divisive politics, falling living standards and dashed hopes.

The job market appears to be increasingly polarized, with high-paid and low-paid occupations growing quickly, while middle-class jobs are disappearing. Labor-saving technological change has, over time, replaced a number of "routine" middle-class jobs like manufacturing, while leaving low-end service jobs and high-end positions largely untouched. There's been a

substantial increase in innovative thinking on the replacement
of human capital. Add to that changes in process to make less
human capital far more productive. So why should anyone
spend any time on using more human capital? The group
which is partially responsible for this are the geeks from Silicon
Valley who told us everything could be 'free' and easy, in a true
vision of virtual utopia (Moore, 2013). If technology could
remove the burden of working and being miserable as a result
than this is what we wanted – less work and more free time. In
the gradual shift from a production economy to a consumption
economy, this was certainly inevitable. People could then
spend their lives pursuing their passions and collaborating on
the next big innovation. In essence everything would become
open source. Why not? For instance John Maynard Keynes in
the 1930s postulated that with technological progress many
countries will experience peace and people will have a lot of
free time. Unfortunately, he was (and he is still) wrong. Others
were wrong too. In the classic cartoon series „The Jetsons"
only the father, George Jetson, worked. His work involved
pressing a button, once if my memory serves me, to switch on
the production line. Maybe during the whole working day he
had to press the button twice, the other time to switch
production off. He provided for a family of four with this job!
When we were children I bet most of us didn't appreciate the
beautiful vision the cartoon's creators were painting before our
eyes. Where's the four-day work week, the increased wages,
better working conditions which the futurists in the 1950s and
60s predicted? The solution to this problem isn't increasingly
pointless work, but a new way of legitimately getting capital
ownership into the hands of the people who now don't have it,
through as we know it – work 2.0 and free access to all
industries as they free themselves from the need for human
labour. Minimal oversight by volunteers is really all that would
be needed. This issue is tackled by Jaron Lanier's book "Who
Owns the Future?", where he argues: "Capitalism only works if
there are enough successful people to be customers" (2013).
That's just another way of saying what Ford said, that cars

won't buy cars (as opposed to people). "One's own employees ought to be one's own best customers" Ford said years later. Lanier and many others claim that we can design a micropayment system for content. But this doesn't necessarily have to be that simple. A micropayment system has to be profitable – and if it were profitable it probably already would have been implemented (with the help of, say, crowdfunding) by now.

The division of labour has gone through two major transitions in human economic history (the Agrarian Revolution and the Industrial Revolution) and is currently undergoing a third transformation, the Cognitive Revolution. The Cognitive Revolution has come about through ongoing technological progress and economic growth, leading in turn to increasing production streamlining and automation and a shift of human employment from producing to cognitive work. However, cognitive work requires an increasing quantity of investment in education to work in World 2.0 – thus the cost of having children rises (they require more initial investment) while the demand for human work falls rapidly (the economy requires a smaller group of highly-skilled cognitive workers rather than exhibiting larger demand for industrial labour, leading to a surplus of unwanted human work, which would have previously been employed in production). Where is this leading us? Some trends may become apparent by studying the last 10 years of the digital reality. Figure 20 offers a comparison of decades in terms of job creation. In the decade of 1970-80 27.6% jobs were created (compound annual jobs growth was nearly 2.5%), in 1980-90 20.2% new jobs were created (compound annual jobs growth was nearly 2%), in the 1990s employment increased by 19.8% (compound annual jobs growth was nearly 1.9%). Meanwhile, the last decade, the years 2000-2010, resulted in a 1.1% job loss in comparison with 2000.

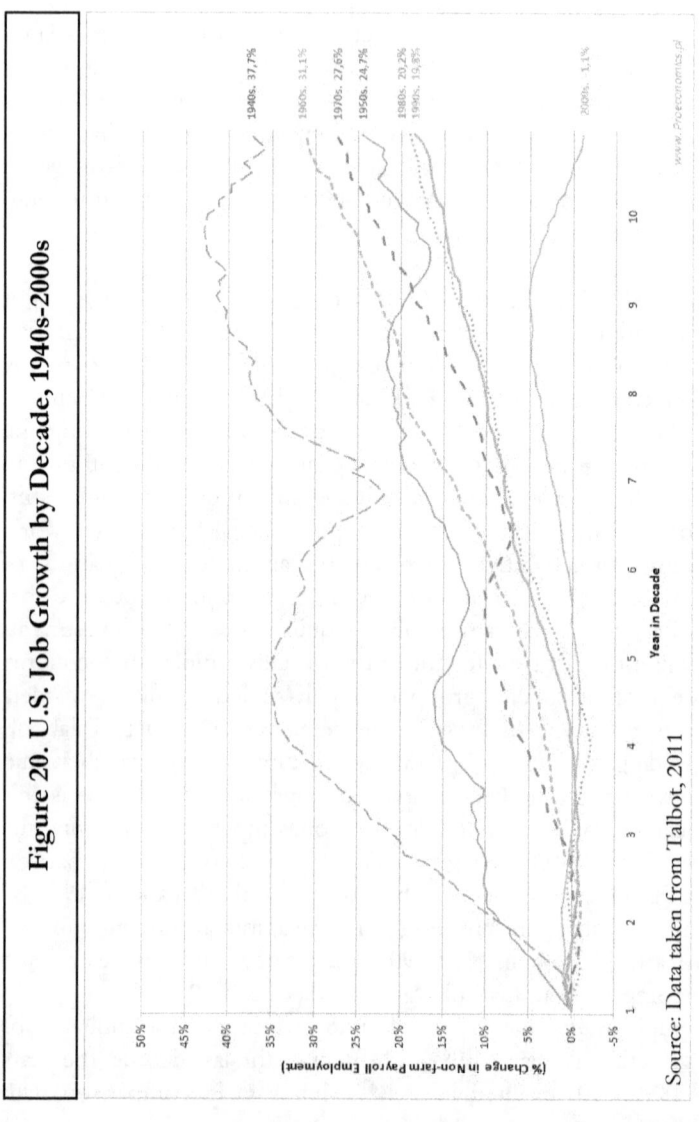

Figure 20. U.S. Job Growth by Decade, 1940s-2000s

Source: Data taken from Talbot, 2011

As we can see from the graph the 2000-2010 decade is a time without precedent in recent history. The number of jobs isn't growing; in fact it's dropping. The phenomenon of Work 2.0 is economic growth without job growth, or even, paradoxically, growth through job destruction. Yet what's most interesting is that this isn't as bad as it seems. Douglas Rushkoff from New York University is of the opinion that the essence of the change is a shift of rules which up to now have governed the market economy. Rushkoff's ideas are based on the economic growth experienced by the West. Since the 19th century we have witnessed global GDP growth by a factor of 80, the average income per inhabitant of planet Earth has risen eleven-fold even with a sevenfold increase in global population. The post-war period, when the foundations were laid for the current lifestyle of our civilisation, saw a 4-5% annual growth rate of mature economies. Internet has completely overturned the rules which have governed the capitalist economy for the last hundreds of years. Before the change, it was based more or less on the rule that rational agents on the market (*homo oeconimicus* if you will) maximise their profits by acquiring and distributing scarce goods, i.e. valuable goods. This has now changed. Classic economists such as Adam Smith or David Ricardo would certainly not consider someone to be rational if he dedicates valuable resources (that is his time and knowledge) on free improvements to Wikipedia or uploading videos to YouTube. Meanwhile the answer to this question is that the Wikipedian or YouTube user makes an effort but in exchange he is happier. We have access to an unimaginable amount of treasure of human cultural heritage, we can tweet what we like, contact our friends on Facebook or upload our photos on Instagram rather than keep them locked up. This makes us happier. This comes with one caveat, Wikipedia or YouTube don't boost consumption, and they don't create many jobs. Thus we see that innovations don't change our reality to better or worse, to use judgemental words, but they certainly do change it.

In their famous book "Race Against the Machine", Erik Brynjolfsson and Andrew McAfee show that the US has become increasingly segregated into the 'haves' and 'have-nots' (2011). For example, in 1977 the top 1%'s share in GDP was 9%. However, in 2007, this share rose to 23%, while the top 0.1%'s share was11%. Furthermore, 50% of the nation's wealth is now controlled by the wealthiest 3% of households.

Just to make this point clear, 400 people have more wealth than 155 million people combined. Paul Buchheit, from DePaul University, found that from 1980 to 2006 the richest 1% in the US tripled their after-tax percentage of the nation's total income, while the bottom 90% have seen a drop of over 20%. Robert Freeman adds: "Between 2002 and 2006, it was even worse: an astounding three-quarters of all the economy's growth was captured by the top 1%" (DeGraw, 2010). William M. Rodgers III reached similar conclusions by comparing the cumulative growth in average inflation-adjusted before-tax incomes (earnings and wages for individuals and family income) for the bottom 99% and top 1%. Although there is significant variability in the sampling and changes in the way the top is defined by the U.S. Census Bureau, greatly expanded income inequality is evident. After the 1991-92 recession, the income growth of the top 1% (individual and family income) accelerated while the income growth of the bottom 99% was more or less stagnant (2012).

**Figure 21. Segregation into the 'haves' and 'have-nots'
according to year's salary in USA (2012)**

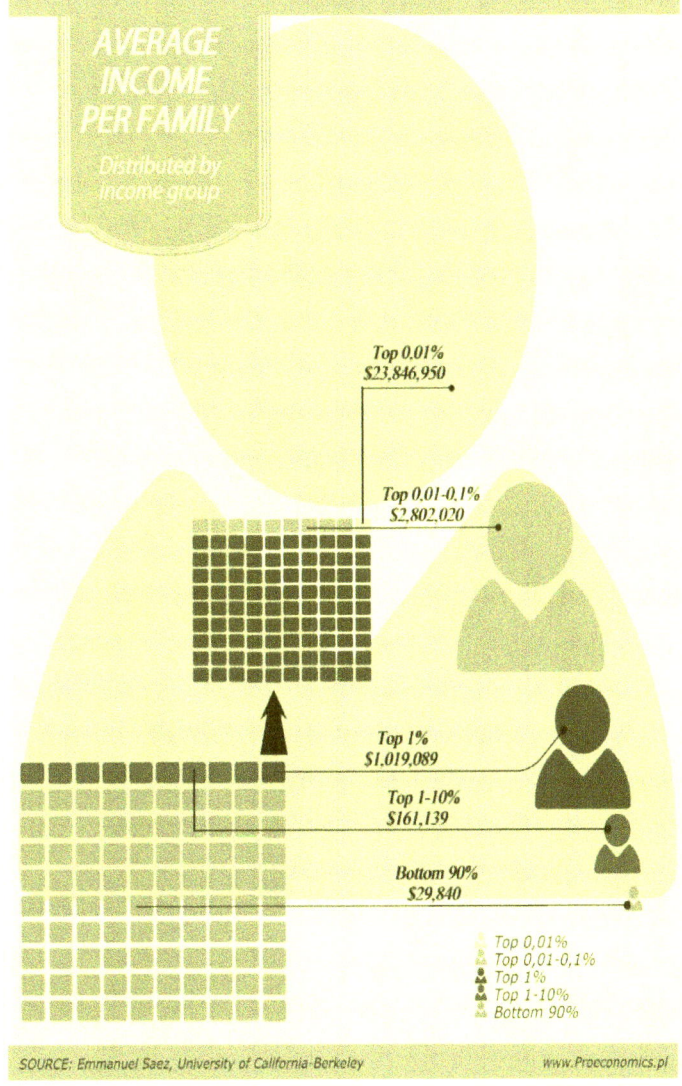

AVERAGE
INCOME
PER FAMILY

Distributed by
income group

Top 0.01%
$23,846,950

Top 0.01-0.1%
$2,802,020

Top 1%
$1,019,089

Top 1-10%
$161,139

Bottom 90%
$29,840

Top 0,01%
Top 0,01-0,1%
Top 1%
Top 1-10%
Bottom 90%

SOURCE: Emmanuel Saez, University of California-Berkeley   www.Proeconomics.pl

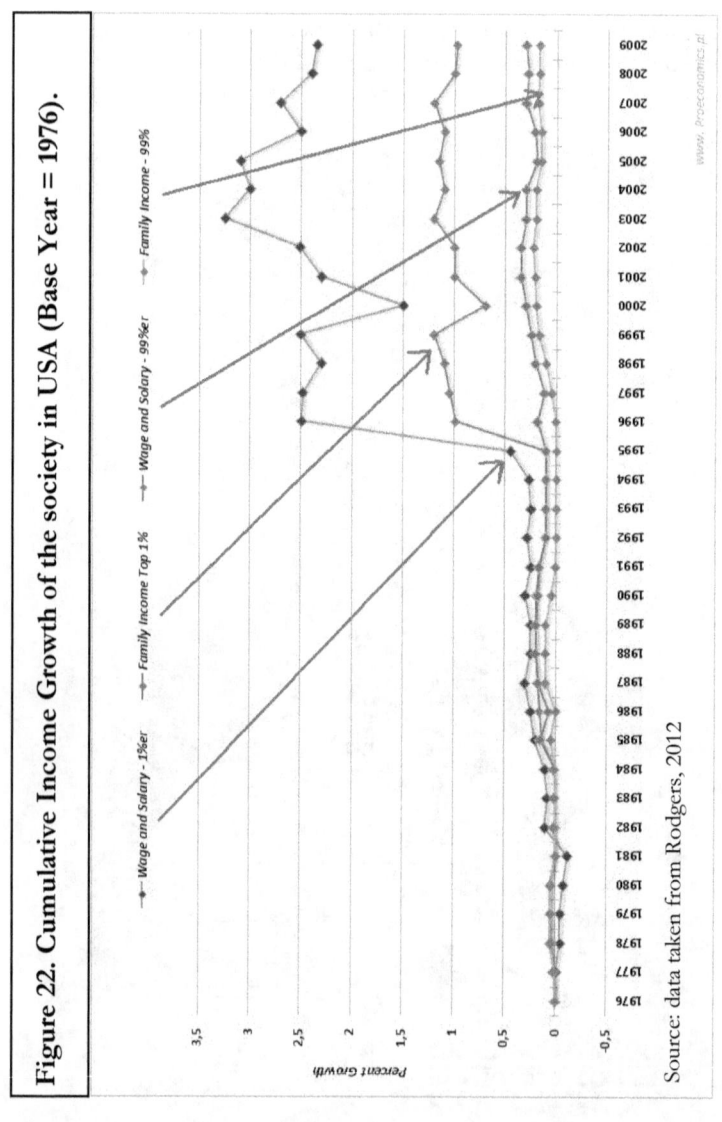

Figure 22. Cumulative Income Growth of the society in USA (Base Year = 1976).

Source: data taken from Rodgers, 2012

McAfee and Brynjolfsson think that technology is partly to blame for the rising income inequality in the US and a stagnant median income since the start of the new century. It's a winner-take-all world, with a tiny number of successful people and everyone else living on hope. This is because the web is perceived to be (and in fact is) a new repository of cheap labour. Hobbyists, amateurs and enthusiasts find work through it, reducing costs and making labour cheaper. This happens from the bottom up – since open source programmers write applications and other software for free, and their quality can compete with (or even surpasses) commercial products made by well-paid corporation employees. But contrary to popular thinking, rich people don't create jobs – consumers do, and corporations and businesses hire to meet the demands of the consumer. If it's an all-or-nothing society the internet may destroy the middle classes--the people who can't outspend the elite. And without that middle group, we cannot maintain a democracy. Thomas Jefferson once said:

"*The democracy will cease to exist when you take away from those who are willing to work and give to those who would not.*" (UVA EText Jefferson Digital Archive, 2013)

Searching for a way out Brynjolfsson and McAfee propose to change the „race against the machine" for the „race with the machine", i.e. creatively use the logic of accelerating technological progress, but this calls for completely rebuilding the educational system and our socio-economic model. Robert Solow sees this problem and calls for profound changes in the post-capitalist society:

"*(…)is how to make an economy that will deal with a situation in which an enormous amount of labor becomes superfluous, in which almost all the work is done by robots, including the manufacture of robots. There you have to begin thinking about how you support a population. One way to do it, of course, would be democratization of capital. If all the income is being earned, in effect, by capital-by machines of one kind or another - then the economy becomes a kind of mutual fund, a situation in which the ownership of all that capital is spread around the population. That is a century away, or two centuries away, or maybe never."* (Talbot, 2011)

One thing is certain, experts are looking for a solution to this socio-economic problem right now. An interesting idea is state subsidies to citizens, whose proponents say it would be a helpful starting point for us to introduce an unconditional BASIC INCOME (Torry, 2013a). The website http://www.basicincome2013.eu/ is gathering e-signatures supporting this idea. What lies at the heart of this concept?

"Everyone gets it; everyone of the same age gets the same amount – whatever our employment status, whatever our income, whatever our household structure, whatever our relationships ... whatever. And it is nonwithdrawable – which means that if we earn additional income then the benefit isn't taken away. If we are on means-tested benefits and we earn additional income then benefits are withdrawn, which means that there is little incentive to earn additional income. A Citizen's Income would not be withdrawn, so there would be far more incentive to seek employment, or to seek new skills, or to seek a better paid job." (Torry, 2013b)

In other words, this is the intended message: "We'll pay you for being a consumer!" It sounds great and I would gladly vote for it (it wouldn't be all that bad having a basic income!), but... I'm still hesitant. Money just doesn't appear from thin air. This idea goes against the incentives needed for productivity and efficiency growth. It would also be another step towards an increased role of the welfare state (which, as opposed to the market, isn't very efficient and needs intermediaries – civil servants) and finally I wonder whether it would be morally acceptable given the situation of the poorest nations. Should a Norwegian, German or American receive more than an Indonesian, Bolivian or Gabonese citizen just because the former live in World 2.0 where there's not enough work to go around while in World 1.0 the latter have to work hours every day in conditions which are far from perfect? The West has become rich thanks to economic and political institutions which encourage economic growth and market development, incentivise hard work, and not handouts. The free market economy is a great and powerful tool. We shouldn't throw it away just yet. The problem the market solves is to maximise the allocation of all goods and resources in order for them to create the most value for society. Without this tool, goods are poorly allocated and used, and great waste is created.

It is usually the case that the fruit of revolution can be consumed after a certain time, which is often two or three decades after the tumultuous times of change. Technologies need time to adapt and find their real meaning, and the biggest barrier of all is overcoming human opportunism and, sometimes, unbridled greed.

CHAPTER 8: CONCLUSIONS. WHAT SHOULD WE DO?

Felippo Tommaso Marinetti wrote in the „Futurist Manifesto", published on the front page of the French newspaper „Le Figaro" on the 20th February 1909, about a vision of man deprived of his natural roots, who is ready to become one with the engine. He wanted to abandon the past and embrace the future. These dreams have been expressed already decades ago by writers and philosophers. Many artificial people were conceived as early as the 19th century, as evidenced by the literary characters such as Pinocchio, Frankenstein and Golem. A hundred years after Marinetti, the British Royal Astronomer, professor Martin Rees, stated that the current 21st century is the last century of man - that in one hundred years machines will drive us out (Rees, 2013). He doesn't necessarily mean just robots, but also computers and computer programmes. It is worth noting one thing at this time – if this were to happen, we would have to assume that the machines desire for it to come about, that there is some kind of mechanism which leads them to want this. Currently no such mechanism exists, so a far more likely scenario is the cooperation of humans with computers at a currently unimaginable level.

How large a scale is this? Andy Warhol and his rock band „Velvet Underground" recorded the hit single „I Want To Be A Machine" by using many traditional instruments. Currently the robotisation of popular music is so far advanced that rather than having the music's author or performer we have computer-developed loops, or machine-repeated sounds coming from computer-generated instruments, or samples – fragments of soundtracks. Sound-like products are being subjected to ever more transformations with the use of algorithms. The artist is becoming only the face of the operation. He depends on computers – without them he won't create anything – he won't 'generate' music. This example ideally relates to one of my favourite sayings about the role of technology in society – Kranzberg's first law, which states, "Technology is neither good nor bad – nor is it neutral". The same applies to capitalism, where technologies reside. Nevertheless, capitalism is endlessly adaptable and will easily adapt to the new world. It will become techno-capitalism, with a central role of the web which reaches every individual.

The internet has created a new world, both dangerous and attractive and interesting. The fetishisation of technology, innovativeness, creativity and creation takes place in this new world. The web has also created the foundations for a new type of work – Work 2.0 – whose workers are characterised by virtuality and disembodiment. Their minds, bodies and identities are informational, flexible, and based on multitasking. As opposed to the traditional Weberian spirit of capitalism, the ideology inscribed into techno-capitalism is its spirit of informationalism. In the new world economy, life is information. The web is the economy.

One thing is clear. You can't refuse to stay out of the digital era. It's becoming a self-serving world. Instead of relying on someone else in the workplace or in our personal lives, we use technology to do the tasks ourselves. Some find this frustrating, while others like the feeling of control. Either way, this trend will only grow as software permeates our lives. Even if you manage to stay out of the digital era, you will be in a negligible minority. So the choice is to either embrace growth and live in utopia or go back to medieval feudalism. What's better? The solution would be obvious in a binary World 2.0 – ban the technology! Burn your laptop or your Kindle! Or, alternatively, stop being a Luddite 2.0 and come to realise that technology's been making somebody's job obsolete since the first wheel rolled down a hill. Find your place in World 2.0. Create you identity. Learn the knowledge only people with a very narrow specialty have and confirm it with a certificate. Focusing on your professional development you must always remember that you should be good at the things where machines don't cope. Machines are great at routine adjustments to different templates, making routine decisions, conducting routine communication. So if these abilities are the basis of your professional career, I think you're in for trouble. We should act completely opposite to the way they do. If your career is based on creativity, the search for innovation, lifelong learning, the need for solving problems and very well-developed interpersonal skills, where many new technologies can provide help, then I don't think anything will be in the way of your professional development.

REFERENCES

Ajilon Professionals (2010), *Future Jobs: How We Will Work in the Europe of the Future*, Ajilon Professionals, available online at: http://www.ajilon.nl/SiteCollectionDocuments/whitepapers/09-White-Paper-Future-Jobs.pdf [accessed 23 Aug. 2013].

Albanesi S., Gregory V., Patterson C., Şahin A. (2013), Is Job Polarization Holding Back the Labor Market?, available online at: http://libertystreeteconomics.newyorkfed.org/2013/03/isjob-polarization-holding-back-the-labor-market.html [accessed 29 Aug. 2013].

Asker, J., Farre-Mensa, J. and Ljungqvist, A. (2013), *Corporate Investment and Stock Market Listing: A Puzzle?*, ECGI Finance Working Paper, April 2013.

Autor, D.H. and Dorn, D. (2011), *The Growth of Low-skill Service Jobs and the Polarization of the U.S. Labor Market*, MIT working paper, June 2011.

Barber, B.R. (2008), *Consumed: How Markets Corrupt Children, Infantalize Adults, and Swallow Citizens Whole*, W.W. Norton & Company.

Bauman, Z. (2008), *The Art of Life*, Polity Press.

Bell, D. (1973), *The Coming of Post-Industrial Society: A Venture in Social Forecasting*, Basic Books.

Bellido, A. (2006), *Telework People: How to Make Money and Get Your Life Back by Working Online*, Lulu.com.

Bernstein, J. and Baker, D. (2003), *The Benefits of Full Employment: When Markets Work for People*, Economic Policy Institute.

Bivens, J. (2011), *Failure by Design: The Story behind America's Broken Economy (An Economic Policy Institute Book)*, ILR Press.

Bollier, D. (2011), *The Future of Work: What It Means for Individuals, Businesses, Markets and Governments*, The Aspen Institute.

Bresnahan, T.F., Brynjolfsson, E. and Hitt, L.M. (2002), 'Information Technology, Workplace Organization and the Demand for Skilled Labour: Firm-Level Evidence', *Quarterly Journal of Economics*, Vol. 118, Feb 2002, pp. 339-376.

Brown, J.S. (2006), *Relearning Learning – Applying the Long Tail to Learning*, Presentation at MIT iCampus, 1 Dec. 2006, available online at: http://mitworld.mit.edu/video/419/ [accessed 23 Aug. 2013].

Brynjolfsson, E. and McAfee, A. (2011), *Race Against The Machine: How the Digital Revolution is Accelerating Innovation, Driving Productivity, and Irreversibly Transforming Employment and the Economy*, Digital Frontier Press.

Bughin, J. and Manyika, J. (2007), 'How Businesses Are Using Web 2.0: A McKinsey Global Survey', *The McKinsey Quarterly*, 20 May 2007, available online at: http://www.skmf.net/fileadmin/redaktion/aktiver_content/0 1_Events/080514_SWISS_KM_Tool_Tag/Track_0_Other_M aterial/0005_How_firms_use_Web20.pdf [accessed 23 Aug. 2013].

Bughin, J., Manyika, J. and Roberts, R. (2008), 'New Degrees of Management Freedom: Challenging Sloan Age Business Orthodoxies', *McKinsey Technology Initiative Perspective*, October 2008.

Bureau of Labor Statistics (2011), *Labor Force Statistics from the Current Population Survey*, United States Department of Labor, available online at: http://www.bls.gov/cps/cpsaat03.htm [accessed 23 Aug. 2013].

Bureau of Labor Statistics (2012a), *Table 5. Employment by major occupational group, 2010 and projected 2020, and median annual wage*, May 2010, modified 1 Feb 2012, available online at: http://bls.gov/news.release/ecopro.t05.htm [acccessed 23 Aug. 2013].

Bureau of Labor Statistics (2012b), *Table 9. Employment and total job openings by education, work experience, and on-the-job training category, 2010 and projected 2020*, modified 1 Feb.2012, available online at: http://bls.gov/news.release/ecopro.t09.htm

Bureau of Labor Statistics (Various years), *Job Openings and Labor Turnover Survey* [database], available online at: http://www.bls.gov/jlt/#data [acccessed 23 Aug. 2013].

Bureau of Economics Analysis, FED, [database], 2013.

Carnot, M. (2002), *Utrwalenie nowej gospodarki*, Toruń.

Castells, M. (1996), *The Rise of the Network Society*, Vol. 1 of *The Information Age: Economy, Society and Culture*, Blackwell Publishing.

Chui, M. and Comes, F. (2011), 'Competing Through Data: Three Experts Offer their Game Plans', *McKinsey Quarterly*, October 2011, available online at: http://www.mckinsey.com/insights/marketing_sales/competing_through_data_three_experts_offer_their_game_plans [accessed 23 Aug. 2013].

Collaboration and collective intelligence [online] (2007), *Presentation for MIT Communications Forum*, 27 April 2007, [accessed 20 May 2008].

Czubkowska, S. (2013), *Internet zabija gospodarkę*, e-Magnes, 3 Apr. 2013, available online at: http://polityka.e-magnes.pl/news.php?extend.1355 [accessed 23 Aug. 2013].

Dawson, R. (2008), *Web 2.0* [blog] [accessed 20 May 2008].

DeGraw, D. (2010), *The Richest 1% Have Captured America's Wealth -- What's It Going to Take to Get It Back?*, AlterNet, 16 Feb. 2010, available online at: http://www.alternet.org/story/145705/the_richest_1_have_captured_america%27s_wealth_--_what%27s_it_going_to_take_to_get_it_back [accessed 23 Aug. 2013].

Dobbs *et al.* (2012), *The World at Work: Jobs, Pay, and Skills for 3.5 Billion People*, McKinsey Global Institute, available online at: http://www.mckinsey.com/insights/employment_and_growth/the_world_at_work [accessed 23 Aug. 2013].

Doeringer, P.B. and Piore, M.J. (1985), *Internal Labor Markets and Manpower Analysis*, M.E. Sharpe.

Drucker, P.F. (1994), *Post-Capitalist Society*, HarperCollins Publishers.

Drucker, P.F. (2005), 'Managing Oneself', *Harvard Business Review*, Jan. 2005.

Edelman, R. (2000), 'Liquid Truth: Advice from the Spinmeisters', *PR Watch*, Vol. 7, No. 4.

Epstein, C.F. (ed.) and Kalleberg, A.L. (ed.) (2006), *Fighting for Time: Shifting Boundaries of Work and Social Life*, Russell Sage Foundation.

Ernst, E. *et al.* (2013), *The Global Employment Trends 2013*, International Labour Organisation, available online at: http://www.ilo.org/wcmsp5/groups/public/---dgreports/---dcomm/---publ/documents/publication/wcms_202326.pdf [accessed 23 Aug. 2013].

Eurostat database, 2012.

Fingar, P. (2007a), *The Greatest Innovation Since BPM*, BPTrends, March 2007, available online at: http://www.bptrends.com/publicationfiles/SIX-03-07-COL-TheGreatestInnovationSinceBPM-Fingar-Final1.pdf [accessed 23 Aug. 2013].

Fingar, P. (2007b), *Work 2.0*, Search: Digital World.

Fisher, E. (2010), *Media and New Capitalism in the Digital Age: The Spirit of Networks*, Palgrave Macmillan.

Fitts, P.M. and Posner, M.I. (1967), *Human Performance*, Brooks/Cole Pub. Co.

Florida, R. (2002), *The Rise of the Creative Class: And How It's Transforming Work, Leisure, Community and Everyday Life*, Basic Books.

Foy, N. (1972), 'Action Learning Comes to Industry', *Harvard Business Review*, Vol. 55, No. 5.

Frank, M. and Moore, G. (2010) *The Future of Work: A New Approach to Productivity and Competitive Advantage*, Cognizant, available online at: http://www.cognizant.com/InsightsWhitepapers/FutureofWork-A-New-Approach.pdf [accessed 23 Aug. 2013].

Frauenheim, E. (2007), 'HR Software Face-Off Reveals Latest Trends', *Workforce Management*, Vol. 86, No. 18, 22 Oct. 2007.

Freeman, C. and Soete, L. (1997), *The Economics of Industrial Revolution*, 3rd edition, Pinter.

Friedman, T. (2000), *The Lexus and the Olive Tree*, Anchor Books.

Friedman, T. (2005), *The World is Flat: A Brief History of the Twenty-first Century*, Farrar, Straus and Giroux.

Giddens, A. (2007), *Europe in the Global Age*, Polity Press.

GlobalWebIndex, https://www.globalwebindex.net/ [accessed 23 Aug. 2013].

Gould, E. (2012), *A Decade of Declines in Employer-Sponsored Health Insurance Coverage*, Economic Policy Institute Briefing Paper No. 337, available online at: http://www.epi.org/publication/bp337-employer-sponsored-health-insurance/ [accessed 23 Aug. 2013].

Government Communication Network (2007), *A Review of the Government's Use of Social Media*, Government Communication Network.

Gratton, L. (2010), 'Forces Shaping the Future of Work', *Business Strategy Review*, 3/2010.

Herzberg, F. (1968), 'One More Time: How Do You Motivate Employees?', *Harvard Business Review Classic*, January-February 1968, available online at: http://gaounion.net/wp-content/uploads/2007/09/196801-02-hbr-herzberg-articleon-motivation.pdf [accessed 8 Feb. 2011].

Hodgkin, P. and Munro, J. (2007), 'The Long Tale: Public Services and Web 2.0', *Consumer Policy Review*, Vol. 17, No. 2, May-Jun. 2007, pp. 84-89.

Hoffman, B. and Casnocha, B. (2012), *The Start-up of You: Adapt to the Future, Invest in Yourself, and Transform Your Career*, Crown Business.

International Telecommunication Union (2013), *World Telecommunication/ICT Indicators database* [database], available online at: http://www.itu.int/en/ITU-D/Statistics/Pages/publications/wtid.aspx [accessed 26 Aug. 2013].

Jarrett, K. (2008), 'Interactivity is Evil! A Critical Investigation of Web 2.0', *First Monday*, Vol. 13, No. 3, 3 Mar. 2008, available online at: http://firstmonday.org/ojs/index.php/fm/rt/printerFriendly/2140/1947#13 [accessed 23 Aug. 2013].

Jensen, B. (2003), *Work 2.0: Building the Future, One Employee At A Time*, Perseus Publishing.

Jung, B. (2010), 'Kreatywne gospodarki i "kreatywna klasa". Otoczenie mediów ery Web 2.0', in: Jung, B., *Wokół mediów ery 2.0*, WAiP.

Kamel Boulos, M.N and Wheeler, S. (2007), 'The Emerging Web 2.0 Social Software" An Enabling Suite of Sociable Technologies in Health and Health Care Education', *Health Information and Libraries Journal*, Vol. 24, No. 1, pp. 2-23.

Kinal, T. and Hypponen, O. (2013), 'Unleashing the Future of Work', *Unleash*, April 2013, available online at: http://unleashteam.com/wp-content/themes/unleash%20v2/pdf/Unleashing.pdf [accessed 23 Aug. 2013].

Kotler, P., Kartajaya, H. and Setiawan, I. (2010), *Marketing 3.0: From Products to Customers to the Human Spirit*, John Wiley & Sons.

Kurtz, H. (2006), 'Loneliness, Lies and Videotapes', *The Washington Post*, 18 Sep. 2006.

Lanier, J. (2013), *Who Owns the Future?*, Simon & Schuster.

Laurel, B. (1993), *Computers as Theatre*, Addison Wesley.

Leadbeater, C. (2009), *We Think: The Power of Mass Creativity*, Profile Books.

Malone, T. (2004), 'The Future of Work', *Research Brief*, No. 1, Vol. 4, Center for eBusiness, MIT, available online at: http://ebusiness.mit.edu/research/Briefs/4Malone_Work_Brief_Final.pdf [accessed 23 Aug. 2013].

Malone, T.W., Laubacher, R.J. and Johns, T. (2011), 'The Age of Hyperspecialization', *Harvard Business Review*, July-August 2011.

Manpower Group (2011), *2011 Talent Shortage Survey Results*, Manpower Group.

Markoff, J. (2011), 'Armies of Expensive Lawyers, Replaced by Cheaper Software', *The New York Times*, 4 Mar. 2011, available online at: http://www.nytimes.com/2011/03/05/science/05legal.html?pagewanted=all&_r=1& [accessed 23 Aug. 2013].

Martin, G. (2009), 'Employer Branding and Corporate Reputation Management: A Model and Some Evidence', in: Burke, R.J. (ed.) and Cooper, C.L. (ed.) (2009), *The Peak Performing Organization (Routledge Research in Strategic Management)*, Routledge.

Martin, G., Reddington, M. and Kneafsey, M.B. (2007), *Web 2.0 and Human Resources*, Chartered Institute of Personnel and Development, available online at: http://www.cipd.co.uk/NR/rdonlyres/38B8F4B5-E83C-4D64-B340-3BB51DA681BB/0/web20andhumanresources.pdf [accessed 23 Aug. 2013].

Mason, R. and Rennie, F. (2007), 'Using Web 2.0 for Learning in the Community, *The Internet and Higher Education*, Vol. 10, No. 3, pp. 196-203.

McAfee, A. "The impact of information technology (IT) on businesses and their leaders [blog].Harvard Business School.[Accessed 20 May 2008].

McKinsey Global Institute, data, 2013.

Milanovic, B. (2012), 'Adam Smiths of Capital, Friedrich Lists of Labor', *The Globalist*, 4 Jun. 2012, available online at: http://www.theglobalist.com/adam-smiths-of-capital-friedrich-lists-of-labor/, [accessed 23 Aug. 2013].

Miller, M. and Miller, J. (2012), 'The Rise of The Supertemp', *Harvard Business Review*, May 2012.

Mishel, L. and Shierholz, H. (2011), 'The Sad But True Story of Wages in America', *Economic Policy Institute Issue Brief*, No. 297,

14 Mar. 2011, available online at:
http://epi.3cdn.net/3b7a1c34747d141327_4dm6bx8ni.pdf
[accessed 23 Aug. 2013].
Mishel, L. and Shierholz, H. (2011), *Sustained, High Joblessness Causes Lasting Damage to Wages, Benefits, Income, and Wealth*, Economic Policy Institute Briefing Paper No. 324, available online
at: http://www.epi.org/publication/sustained_high_joblessnes s_causes_lasting_damage_to_wages_benefits_income_a/
[accessed 23 Aug. 2013].
Mishel, L., Bernstein, J. and Shierholz, H. (2009), *State of Working America: 2008–2009: An Economic Policy Institute Book.*, Cornell University Press.
Mishel, L., Bernstein, J. and Shierholz, H. (forthcoming), *State of Working America, 12th Edition: An Economic Policy Institute Book.*, Cornell University Press.
Moore, S. (2013), 'In the Digital Economy We'll Soon All Be Working For Free – And I Refuse', *The Guardian*, 5 Jun. 2013, available online at:
http://www.theguardian.com/commentisfree/2013/jun/05/di gital-economy-work-for-free [accessed 23 Aug. 2013].
Naisbitt, J. (1982), *Megatrends. Ten New Directions Transforming Our Lives*, Warner Books.
O'Reilly, T. (2005), *What is Web 2.0*, O'Reilly – Spreading the Knowledge of Innovators, available online at:
http://oreilly.com/web2/archive/what-is-web-20.html
[accessed 23 Aug. 2013].
O'Reilly, T. and Battelle, J., *State of the Internet Industry*, San Francisco, California, 5 Oct. 2004, available only at:
http://oreilly.com/web2/archive/what-is-web-20.html
[accessed 23 Aug. 2013].
OECD (2012), *Education at a Glance 2012: Indicators*, OECD Publishing.
Palmer, D. (2003), *The Paradox of User Control*, paper presented at the Fifth International Digital Arts and Culture Conference, Melbourne, Australia, 19-23 May 2003, available online at:

http://hypertext.rmit.edu.au/dac/papers/Palmer.pdf [accessed 23 Aug. 2013].

Pew Research Centre analysis of the Decenial Census, data, 2011.

Pickard, J. and Rigby, E. (2013), 'UK Workers Feel Pain of Years of Falling Wages', Financial Times, 6 Aug. 2013.

Pink, D.H. (2009), *Drive: The Surprising Truth About What Motivates Us*, Penguin Group.

Prahalad, C.K. and Krishnan, M.S. (2008), *The New Age of Innovation: Driving Cocreated Value Through Global Networks*, McGraw-Hill.

R.A. (2011), *Technological Unemployment: Race Against the Machine*, Free Exchange, 9 Nov. 2011, available online at: http://www.economist.com/blogs/freeexchange/2011/11/technological-unemployment [accessed 23 Aug. 2013].

Rees, M. (2003), *Our Final Century?: Will the Human Race Survive the Twenty-first Century?*, William Heinemann Ltd.

Reich, R.B. (1992), *The Work of Nations: Preparing Ourselves for 21st Century Capitalism*, Vintage.

Rifkin, J. (1996), *The End of Work: The Decline of the Global Labor Force and the Dawn of the Post-Market Era*, Tarcher.

Rifkin, J. (2001), *The Age of Access: The New Culture of Hypercapitalism, Where All of Life is a Paid-for Experience*, Penguin Putnam.

Rodgers III, W.M. (2012), *Future Work 2.0: Life After the Great Recession*, John J. Heldrich Center for Workforce Development Working Paper, available online at: http://www.heldrich.rutgers.edu/sites/default/files/content/Future_Work_Report.pdf [accessed 23 Aug. 2013]

RTG (2013), *Update #23: The Director's Cut*, 4 Mar. 2013, Kickstarter, available online at: http://www.kickstarter.com/projects/redthread/dreamfall-chapters-the-longest-journey/posts/419653 [accessed 23 Aug. 2013].

Rybiński, K. (2006), *Globalizacja w trzech odsłonach*, Rybinski.eu – economy of the XXI century, available online at: http://www.rybinski.eu/wp-content/uploads/globalizacja_cz3_061119.pdf [accessed 23 Aug. 2013].

Saez E., University of California-Berkeley, data, 2012, available online at: http://elsa.berkeley.edu/~saez/ [accessed 23 Aug. 2013].

Schmitt, J. (2012), *Health-insurance Coverage for Low-wage Workers, 1979-2010 and Beyond*, paper prepared for the conference 'What Works for Workers? Public Policies and Innovative Strategies for Low-Wage Workers, Georgetown University, 23-24 Feb 2012, available online at: http://www.cepr.net/documents/publications/health-low-wage-2012-02.pdf [accessed 23 Aug. 2013].

Schmitt, J. and Jones, J. (2012), 'Low-wage Workers are Older and Better Educated than Ever', *Center For Economic Policy and Research Issue Brief*, April 2012, available online at: http://www.cepr.net/documents/publications/min-wage3-2012-04.pdf [accessed 23 Aug. 2013].

Schumpeter, J.A. (1934), *The Theory of Economic Development: An Inquiry into Profits, Capital, Credit, Interest, and the Business Cycle*, Transaction Publishers.

Sentier Research, database, 2013.

Shierholz, H. (2012a), *Weaker Jobs Report Is a Reminder that We're Still on a Rocky Road*, Economic Policy Institute Jobs Picture, April 2012, available online at: http://www.epi.org/publication/2012-04-jobs-picture/ [accessed 23 Aug. 2013].

Shierholz, H. (2012b.), *U.S. Labor Market Starts 2012 with Solid Positive Signs but Fewer Jobs than It Had 11 Years Ago*, Economic Policy Institute Jobs Picture, Feb. 2012, available online at: http://www.epi.org/publication/labor-market-starts-2012-solid-positive/ [accessed 23 Aug. 2013].

Shuen, A. (2008), *Web 2.0: A Strategy Guide: Business Thinking and Strategies behind Successful Web 2.0 implementations*, O'Reilly Media.

Sparreboom, T. *et al.* (2013), *Global Employment Trends for Youth 2013*, International Labour Organisation, available online at: http://www.ilo.org/wcmsp5/groups/public/---dgreports/---

dcomm/documents/publication/wcms_212423.pdf [accessed 23 Aug. 2013].

State of Working America (2011a), *Pension Coverage Declines and Gap Widens by Race*, An Economic Policy Institute chart, modified 13 Jan. 2011, available online at: http://stateofworkingamerica.org/charts/private-sector-employer-provided-pension-coverage-1979-2009/ [accessed].

State of Working America (2011b), *Unionization Declines Slowly and Then More Quickly*, An Economic Policy Institute chart, updated 7 Jan. 2011, available online at: http://www.stateofworkingamerica.org/charts/view/43 [accessed].

State of Working America (2011c), *Income for Working-age Households Drops More than 10% in the* 2000s, An Economic Policy Institute chart, updated 1 Dec. 2011, available online at: http://stateofworkingamerica.org/charts/real-median-household-income/ [accessed 23 Aug. 2013].

Surowiecki, J. (2005), *The Wisdom of the Crowds*, Anchor Books.

Syedain, H. (2008), 'Out of This World', *People Management*, Vol. 14, No. 8, 17 Apr. 2008, pp. 20-24.

Talbot, D. (2011), 'How IT Costs More Jobs Than It Creates', *MIT Technology Review*, 25 Oct. 2011, available online at: http://www.technologyreview.com/news/425910/how-it-costs-more-jobs-than-it-creates/ [accessed 23 Aug. 2013].

Tapscott, D. (2006), *Winning with the Enterprise 2.0*, New Paradigm Learning Corporation, available online at: http://web.dubaichamber.ae/LibPublic/Winning%20with%20the%20enterprise%202.0.pdf [accessed 23 Aug. 2013].

Tapscott, D. (2009), *Grown Up Digital: How the Net Generation is Changing Your World*, McGraw-Hill.

The Economist, 'Higher Education: Not What it Used to be', 29 Nov. 2012b, available online at: http://www.economist.com/news/united-states/21567373-american-universities-represent-declining-value-money-their-students-not-what-it [accessed 23 Aug. 2013].

The Economist, 'Learning New Lessons', 19 Dec. 2012a, available online at:

http://www.economist.com/news/international/21568738-online-courses-are-transforming-higher-education-creating-new-opportunities-best [accessed 23 Aug. 2013].

The Economist, 'Youth Unemployment: Generation Jobless', 27 Apr. 2013, available online at: http://www.economist.com/news/international/21576657-around-world-almost-300m-15-24-year-olds-are-not-working-what-has-caused, [accessed 23 Aug. 2013].

Thurow, L.C. (1996), *The Future of Capitalism: How Today's Economic Forces Shape Tommorrow's World*, Penguin Books.

Tierney, C., Cottle, S. and Jorgensen, K. (2012), *GovCloud: The Future of Government Work: A GovLab Idea*, Deloitte University Press, available online at: http://cdn.dupress.com/wp-content/uploads/2012/01/DUP118_GovCloud.pdf, [accessed 23 Aug. 2013].

Toffler, A. (1989), *The Third Wave*, Bantam Books.

Torry, M. (2013a), *Money for Everyone: Why We Need A Citizen's Income*, Policy Press.

Torry, M. (2013b), *A Podcast About the New Book: 'Money for Everyone: Why We Need A Citizen's Income'*, Citizen's Income Trust, 17 Jun. 2013, available online at: http://citizensincome.blogspot.co.uk/2013/06/a-podcast-about-new-book-money-for.html [accessed 23 Aug. 2013].

U.S. Census Bureau (2011), *Poverty Thresholds for 2010 by Size of Family and Number of Related Children Under 18 Years*, available online at: http://www.census.gov/hhes/www/poverty/data/threshld/thresh10.xls [acccessed 23 Aug. 2013].

U.S. Census Bureau (various years) *Current Population Survey Outgoing Rotation Group microdata*S [machine-readable microdata file] available online at: http://www.bls.census.gov/cps_ftp.html#cpsbasic [accessed].

UVA EText Jefferson Digital Archive, *Jeffersonian Cyclopedia, Thomas Jefferson on Politics and Government, Texts by or to Thomas Jefferson from the Modern English Collection*, available online at: http://guides.lib.virginia.edu/TJ#jeffersoncollections [accessed 23 Aug. 2013].

Vistage (2011), *The Future of Work: How the New Order of Work is Permanently Changing and Reshaping the Future of Small Business*, Vistage. White Paper, available online at:
http://www.vistage.com/media/pdfs/future-of-Work.pdf [accessed 23 Aug. 2013].

Weisbrod, M.R. (2004), *Productive Workplaces Revisited: Dignity, Meaning, and Community in the 21st Century*, Jossey-Bass.

Wiseman, P. and Washington, J. (2013), 'U.S. Labor Force Participation Rate Lowest Since 1979', *Huffington Post*, 6 Apr. 2013, available online:
http://www.huffingtonpost.com/2013/04/06/labor-force-participation-rate_n_3028135.html [accessed 23 Aug. 2013].

Zammuto, R.F., Griffith, T.L. and Majchrzak, A. (2007), 'Information Technology and the Changing Fabric of Organization', *Organization Science*, Vol. 18, No. 5, Sep-Oct 2007, pp. 749-762.

LIST OF FIGURES AND TABLES

SERGIUSZ PROKURAT

AUTHOR'S NOTE TO READERS

Dear Readers,
I would like to thank you for choosing this book. I would very much like to get to know your opinions about Work 2.0. If you have any thoughts about the book, I'd like to ask you to send them to: sergiusz.prokurat@gmail.com.

I'm waiting for your feedback.

Thanks again!

ABOUT THE AUTHOR

Sergiusz Prokurat – Historian, Economist. Economics and project management lecturer at the Alcide Gaspari University of Euroregional Economy in Poland. Lecturer at the MBA study programme organised by ISG Paris and EUE. Director of the Poland-Asia Research Center think tank, based in Warsaw. Independent economics, business expert and consultant with many academic and commercial projects. In the past, he worked for Citibank, BDO, Harvard Business Review. Currently a PhD candidate at the Polish Academy of Science. Hold a Wiener Institut/PAN MBA degree. Also hold numerous professional certificates (PMP, PRINCE2 Foundation, PRINCE2 Practitioner, ITIL Foundation, MOR Foundation). His opinions, articles were published in: „Harvard Business Review", „National Geographic Traveler", „Wprost", „Gazeta Bankowa", „Gazeta Finansowa", „Metropolia Bussiness Magazine", „Rynki Zagraniczne", „Stosunki Międzynarodowe", „Mówia Wieki", "Proseed", „Nowy Dziennik", "Najwyższy Czas", „Dziennik Gazeta Prawna", „Focus Historia", He's blogging at proeconomics.pl

"For some time now I have been interested in the transformation taking place in the economy and at the workplace – a shift I could experience working for Harvard Business Review and interviewing leading thinkers of business and economic studies. I decided to write the book "Work 2.0." to share my insights and knowledge which I gained throughout this extraordinary front-seat learning process".

**Book has a dedicated website in english
work-2-0.com**

www.ingramcontent.com/pod-product-compliance
Lightning Source LLC
Chambersburg PA
CBHW051313170526
45166CB00002B/531